FINDING YOUR PLACE AFTER DIVORCE

FINDING YOUR PLACE AFTER DIVORCE

Help & Hope for Women Who Are Starting Again

Carole Sanderson Streeter

Harold Shaw Publishers
Wheaton, Illinois

Cover design by David LaPlaca

Cover photo © 1992 by Luci Shaw

ISBN 0-87788-269-X

Library of Congress Cataloging-in-Publication Data

Streeter, Carole Sanderson.
    Finding your place after divorce: help and hope for women
  who are starting again / Carole Sanderson Streeter ; foreword
  by David Seamands.
      p.   cm.
    Includes bibliographical references.
    ISBN 0-87788-269-X
      1. Divorced women—United States—Psychology.
  2. Separation (Psychology)   3. Divorce—Religious aspects—
  Christianity.
    I. Title.
  HQ834.S77   1992
  155.6'433—dc20   92-23734
                                                  CIP

99 98 97 96 95 94 93 92

10 9 8 7 6 5 4 3 2 1

For my children—
Catherine Streeter Parker
William Bradford Streeter

CONTENTS

FOREWORD

Those of us who work as pastors and counselors have long been aware of the painful process involved in recovering from divorce.

In recent years we have observed increasing numbers of a particular kind of casualty from this battleground of the broken home—the divorced Christian mother. Her pain is all the greater when the tragedy occurs in the latter years of young adulthood or in mid-life. The intricacies and complexities of the longer years of married life and the older ages of the children make it all the more difficult.

The saddest part of all is the fact that Christian friends and the church often add to the problem rather than help to provide the comfort and support so desperately needed.

For a long time, we have needed a book that deals with this entire problem in complete honesty, without bitterness, and from a fully Christian perspective.

In this excellent book, Carole Streeter has filled that need. Writing from the inside as one who has gone through the shock and trauma of such an experience, she shares her deepest feelings at each step—the loneliness, the guilt, the misunderstandings, the unintended yet hurtful innuendoes from Christians who have never discovered the difference between acceptance and approval, and the confusing and contradictory emotions of the children. All these are accurately and empathically described.

But she does more than "weep with those who weep." She gives comfort, advice, and, best of all, practical suggestions for recovery and healing. Her outlines of the immediate, short-term, and long-term goals are extremely helpful.

This book will be of great value not only to the "wounded" but also to those who try to minister to them.

David A. Seamands

Dean of the Chapel
Asbury Theological Seminary

PREFACE

East of Pastasa is a small Ecuadorian village called Puyupungu. If you climb to the high point at the edge of the village, you can see the reason for its name. *Pungu* is a Quechua word meaning "junction." Looking down from the promontory, you can see the joining of two rivers, the Pastasa and the Puyu. The brown water from the Puyu and the green water from the Pastasa blend slowly. For some distance the two waters flow in a striped effect—a strange sight and yet symbolic of things that happen in our lives. For we have junction points, times of coming together with widely disparate people. And the eventual joining makes all the difference to the rest of our lives.

To the molecules of water, the mingling could seem pointless. But for you, standing high on the ridge, it has meaning because you see the whole picture. You see the river beyond and the mountains in the distance and the blue sky.

Sometimes we feel like the waters of those rivers, being rushed together with persons so different from who we are, even in the intimacies of the home. Yet we know that God is standing on the high point, present at the junctions in our lives. And God, who sees the entire picture, understands the future meanings of those blendings.

I wrote those words in 1969, after spending three days in the jungle village of Puyupungu, visiting my friend Mary Skinner, a missionary from England.

The rather romantic envisioning of the rivers would be a wonderful picture of marriage—the man and the woman slowly blending their lives, overseen, and blessed by the Maker of the marriage oneness.

But wait. You aren't married anymore. Pull back the rivers. Separate the Puyu from the Pastasa. Reverse the flow of waters already so long in mingled flow. Impossible? Yes.

And yet something like this is happening to you. Your part of the river is a maelstrom of angry confusion, and there is no longer any way to tell which molecules of water belonged to you in the beginning. They have all become one, and the undoing of the blending would take forever.

The analogy breaks down, of course, because you are more than molecules of water. But to unmingle ten or twenty years of marriage is as difficult as reversing the flow of water and time in the Puyu and Pastasa.

Which brings up the question—is God present at the breaking points in our lives? Is he here when the even flow becomes a maelstrom? And what does he do about lives that were deliberately blended, now only to be pulled apart? What does God do about one flesh that is ripped in two? With a woman who now feels shredded?

If you are asking these questions about your own life, then this book is for you.

Carole Sanderson Streeter

Wilmore, Kentucky
1992

A NOTE ABOUT THE EXERCISES

Each chapter in this book ends with a short exercise for you to complete. Use them—the book will be more effective if you do. And keep these suggestions in mind:

—**Be honest.** Maybe, when it comes to putting something on paper, you'll be tempted to pretty things up a bit. Don't give in to that temptation. If you feel like your life is a mess, say so. If you think someone was a traitor to you, say that too. You'll be the only one to read what you write here, and it's dangerous to withhold the truth from yourself. Be honest even if it hurts.

—**Be specific.** Whether you're charting goals for your personal life or career or deciding how to accomplish those goals, be specific. Yes, you'll probably change your plans over the coming months and years—but that's what plans are for. The more specific you are now about your present life as well as your future goals, the better you'll be able to decide how appropriate your plans are.

—**Hold yourself accountable for what you write.** If, for instance, at the end of chapter six, you identify hurts that you need to resolve, work at resolving them. They *need* attention. Much of what you will reveal can be considered your own cries for help—help from the Lord and from yourself. Respond as conscientiously as you would to your child's cries for help.

—**Complete the exercises *expectantly***—that is, expecting that this is the beginning of healing for you. It's been a long, rocky road down for you. The road up can be just as rocky—but at least it's up. In the exercises don't regret honestly admitting how difficult things are for you right now. In a year, you should be able to say just as honestly how much better they've become.

CHAPTER ONE

LIFE AMONG THE BREAKAGE

We carry with us the wonders we
seek without us.

—*Sir Thomas Browne*

Cast all your anxiety on him because
he cares for you.

—*1 Peter 5:7*

I left work early that winter afternoon, drove to Oak-
brook to pick up my friend Nancy, and went on to
Chicago to spend the evening with our friends, the
Springers. After we had parked the car and were walking
toward Joe and Betty's home, Nancy turned to me and said,
"I feel so fragile."

Looking at her, I realized how much I had forgotten of
that terrible feeling of vulnerability and defenselessness. I
was eighteen months away from my divorce and had
gained more strength than I knew. Nancy was still too close
to hers and was shaky. I remembered how it had been for
me, not knowing whether I could get through any given
occasion or even whether I had the courage to face it. I

remembered the awful trepidation of meeting people for the first time after the divorce and wondering, "Do they know? How involved is this conversation going to get? Can I control myself?"

Nancy's words and the expression on her face told me to be very careful not to say anything that might add to her feeling of defenselessness.

When I first embarked on the writing of this book, I was five years away from my divorce, and certain wrongs and hurts didn't bother me anymore. That told me that I was about healed. But five years is a big chunk out of anyone's life.

I didn't think much anymore about the year before and after the divorce. But if I tried—as I had to in writing this book—I could feel again the fragility and insecurity of that threatening time. It was during that vulnerable period that my friend Rowena said to me, "You feel shredded." She knew. She too was divorced. And as I pictured limp strips of carrot in a bowl, I thought, "Yes, that's it. What once was strong is now weak and fragmented."

If you're in the early stages of divorce or if you have just gone through a divorce, you too know this fragile feeling. And it can be especially terrible for you if you married once-for-life, with no thought of divorce. That's how it was for Nancy, and that's how it was for me. Divorce just wasn't in the script for our lives. It wasn't done in our families. It was against our Christian faith.

And only when it became a matter of emotional and mental survival for the children and me did I finally take some action. Yes, I filed for divorce. And this is considered by some a reprehensible act. I honestly believe that certain people would have preferred to see me dead.

Divorce is always a failure. Yet in exceptional cases it is necessary. But my having to initiate the divorce action didn't help my feeling of fragility at all. My whole world was breaking apart, and it looked as if I was making it happen. While that was far from true, and while I knew that I was doing the necessary and responsible thing, I also knew that most people would not understand, for I refused to tell very much.

Nor do I plan to go into the painful details here. The telling would not help you and could even hinder you from facing your own problems. Some women see their lives as continuing soap operas. The worse things get, the more they tell. I hope you don't view your life this way.

There is value in those old-fashioned qualities of privacy, loyalty, dignity, and protection of those near to us. I do not believe that we have the right publicly to expose and catalog the sins of other people any more than they have a right to do so to us. And that protection keeps our children from being robbed of their privacy too. We lose nothing—and gain a great deal—if we keep private concerns within a circle of our family and friends.

When, after so many years of marriage, I saw the beginning of the end, I still took a long time to decide. I talked with a psychologist for six months, was in touch with a pastor at our church about once a week, and sought help in other directions.

I am glad, now, that I exhausted all possible resources for help until I was finally convinced that there was no other way. In the years to come, I would need the reassurance that I had done what was necessary, that I had acted responsibly, and that there really was no other alternative.

If you are considering divorce or if you are in the middle of it, please don't proceed until you have exhausted all the other options. And this means that you stay with the helping people for a long period of time, so that they can really understand the conflicts. I have heard people say that they went for counseling (meaning three or four sessions) and that they consulted a pastor (meaning one or two conversations). They are only kidding themselves if they think this means they tried to get help. And they are giving the clear impression that what they really want is to get out of their marriage.

Three Losses

When you are "living among the breakage," a graphic phrase from T.S. Eliot's *The Four Quartets*, what do you do about the feelings of fragility? Of defenselessness? Of instability?

For one thing, you recognize that they are normal. You are devastated and wounded and bleeding. Most of your life has crumbled. You would be less than sane if you were not in turmoil and feeling extremely fragile.

Then, difficult as it is, you need to try to identify what you have lost. Those losses take many forms. In this section I describe three of them, your probable feelings about them, and what you now need.

Loss of place

Places are not only buildings and towns and fields. Places can be emotional spaces. One person finds place in another. God made a place for us, a place of belonging. Then he ordained that we make places for each other.

In a real marriage, a husband feels an aloneness in the inner regions of his being and wants a wife to fulfill those places for him. As he makes a place for her, he finds a place in what she is.

You may not have had what you would call "a real marriage," and yet you had something, more than you thought at times. Now you are displaced. You are without a husband and are experiencing emotional loss. You have no reference point anymore, as in "I'll check with my husband," or "I'll do this because my husband will like it." Your primary position in the inner placings of life is gone. The walls are knocked down. The roots are pulled up. All the defenses are taken away. And there you stand, among the breakage of what was, feeling insecure, emotionally bereft, alone, guilty, not knowing where to turn or what to do first.

You even wonder about the ground you are standing on—it may give way as everything else has. Even assuming you can find a safe place to stand, how do you begin to assemble a whole life, particularly when fifteen, twenty, or twenty-five years of your adult life are past?

Loss of purpose

You fulfill certain roles in society. Everyone does. And those continuing roles help to define you, not only to other people but also to yourself. You have based your goals and your intentions on them.

Now you have lost some of those roles. And when you lost them, you also experienced a loss of will. You are in despair. You feel rejected; you wonder whether you have any meaning in society. You may see your life as futile. You feel dysfunctional and guilty.

All the inner and outer walls of your life have cracked, and many have crumbled. You wonder where you will find the strength to build a new structure for your life—whether you can even figure out how to do it.

You will keep in perfect peace
him whose mind is steadfast,
because he trusts in you.
Trust in the LORD forever,
for the LORD, . . . is the Rock eternal.
—Isaiah 26:3-4

Loss of people

Many of the people you have contact with are determined by your place and purpose in society. For instance, you see relatives because most families get together occasionally. Now you are losing many of the relatives on your husband's side. And those on your side may keep their distance for a while.

Before the divorce you probably saw other couples socially or you got together with groups of families. Now, if you continue to socialize with couples, it will not be with a husband. If you and your children attend functions planned for families, you will be painfully aware of your incompleteness.

Because so many of your acquaintances are afraid of difficult problems, of the irregular or abnormal, most of them will tend to give you a wide berth. Some will refuse to have you in their homes. As you feel the rejection of some people you thought were your friends, you will feel angry, disoriented, and confused.

Because you often see these people, you may dread activities that were once routine. You may be fearful of the unknown, even to the smallest details, and you may wonder whether you'll be able to reestablish some of the old patterns of living or find new routines that will satisfy. You may wonder whether you can continue with some of your friends or whether you will have to start all over with new relationships.

A Place for You

When your life is thrown into crisis, you have the unsought opportunity to learn the practical meaning of ideas that were largely theoretical before. When life is proceeding smoothly, you don't think much about the need for a rock to cling to, for a firm foundation on which to build your future. But when everything around is "shifting sand," as the hymn says, you rapidly realize that you need the stability of a base that isn't going to move.

And nowhere is that more obvious, during this time when you are weak and struggling to work on a dozen different problems at once, than in those areas of your life that are out of your control.

Forget about trying to control the behavior of other people. Forget about trying to manipulate God. Forget about looking for shortcuts to wholeness and healing. There aren't any. Forget about trying to appear fully like other people. You aren't.

You can even forget about insisting that you control your feelings, since you can't anyway. There is too much turmoil right now.

However, you can control three things. The first is your choice of a foundation on which you will build your life. The second is the structure or purpose you give to your life. And the third is your day-to-day behavior.

These three are so vital that you cannot ignore any one of them if you want to come out of this grief whole and productive. And to control your basis for life, your purpose, and your behavior is a fairly full agenda for the first year.

In the best of times, it is hard to admit weakness and inadequacy. Even now, in the worst of times, it is difficult. And yet one of the blessings of a situation that brings you to the end of your resources is that perhaps for the first time you clearly see the all-sufficiency and strength of God.

For the first time, you reach for the solid rock with a faith you have never known before. For the first time, you begin to see yourself as God sees you, and you may even think that you hear him say just to you, "My strength is made perfect in your weakness. My grace is sufficient for you. Take my strength as your own."

I remember several times telling God, "I just don't have what it takes for this conflict. I'm not up to it." Then I imagined him smiling and saying to me, "That's nothing new. But you finally get the point."

My hope is built on nothing less
Than Jesus' blood and righteousness;
I dare not trust the sweetest frame,
But wholly lean on Jesus' name.

When darkness veils His lovely face,
I rest on His unchanging grace;
In every high and stormy gale,
My anchor holds within the veil.

On Christ the solid Rock I stand;
All other ground is sinking sand,
All other ground is sinking sand.

My Hope Is Built on Nothing Less

Foundation

Divorce can bring to light the basics of your own human nature. While this may seem to pull you down at first, it has the effect of lifting up your potential far beyond any level you have previously known. Within this process, there are no easy answers. But one thing I know for sure is that you must get hold of that rock, that foundation, and pull yourself up on it and determine to stay there, come hell or high water. And both will come.

Commit your soul to a faithful Creator and ask him to keep you securely attached to that Rock, which is Christ, the only adequate foundation.

He is the one with whom you deal, first, last, and always. He is the beginning, the end, and the center of everything. Christ is the one who keeps the world from flying apart. And Christ keeps *you* from coming apart. For in him you live and move and have your being. He is before all things, in all things, under and over and around all things, that in all he might have the supremacy.

You can experience his loving strength, his stable compassion, and the demands of discipleship that he places upon you, even in this most difficult time of your life. For the rules don't change when you are in pain. God is not an indulgent babysitter. He is not a bogus shepherd of the sheep. Rather, he presses his demands at times when you will listen. And the chances are good that you are listening better now than you have for a long time. Pain has a way of sharpening your senses. Need makes you reach out for resources you felt no need of before.

If you decide to build and rebuild your life on the only foundation worthy of the name, then all you do in the future will reflect that stability and sureness.

Structure

The main focus of this book is on the kinds of decisions you make in months and years to come. The structure you give to your life will show up in your appointment calendar and in your checkbook, in the work you do, the people you see, the obligations you assume, the roles you fill, the priorities you set, the things you do for relaxation. If you make these decisions based on a growing understanding of the Word of God, you will experience an increasing confidence that you are walking in the truth.

Behavior

Those feelings that we referred to—ebbing and flowing like the waves of the ocean—don't need to worry you if you are determined to control your behavior. You can control where you go, what people you see, what you say, the work you do. You can decide that some behaviors just aren't appropriate for a woman who is basing her life on the foundation of Christ. You can decide that you will not defile yourself, that you will not go against your conscience. Oh, you'll feel like it. You'll feel like doing a lot of things that would make the scandal sheets. But there is no need to act on those feelings.

If you determine that pleasing and obeying God is the primary goal of your life and that you can control your behavior, you will make it through the first year and more in one piece. And you will eventually see your feelings line up with what you have decided to do. This is not to say that living this way is easy, because it's not. And you will have times of loneliness and questioning. But suppose you decide to give in to your impulses. You will still have loneliness and questioning, not to mention guilt, shame, and deep contradiction within yourself.

Every choice excludes something. Every choice sets you farther on the path you have determined. And it is essential that you understand how the choices you make now will determine not only the kind of woman you will be five or fifteen years from now but also the kind of mother your children will have.

God honors the intentions of our hearts. Granted, we don't live up to all of them. But the woman with high purposes to please and obey God is going to come out miles ahead of the woman who just lets things happen, who acts as the perpetual victim, never able to figure out what is happening now, much less what she wants to happen in the future. Such a person is called double-minded in the Scriptures and is characterized by perpetual confusion. But the person who makes it her business to know God increases in strength and senses the validation of the image of God within her.

A Place with a View

I have a favorite stretch of beach along Lake Michigan, near Muskegon, Michigan. It is part of the Maranatha Bible Conference, a place I went for five years as a child, again during college years, and several times when my children were growing up.

One May afternoon while on a business trip, I took a few hours to drive over to Maranatha for some time on the beach and the dunes above. The day was warm, and for about an hour I lay on the sand, basking in the sun and the sounds of the water.

Then I climbed up the wooded dunes to the prayer tower that looks out over the lake. There I was reminded of the importance of perspective. While down on the beach, I got the close-up of sun, wind, water, and a constant reminder of the boundary that a beach is. Up in the tower, I was farther away from the particulars and yet more able to see the whole picture, the long view, not only of the elements of nature but also of my life.

You too need to see your life in a new perspective. You will see how today fits into the whole picture. You will see that your life is greater than your present pain. You will discover new opportunities. You will understand better the perspective of other people.

A woman who rebuilds her life on the sure foundation of Christ is in a secure position from which she is free to discover the many aspects of her life in different lights and seek out those opportunities that she might otherwise miss.

As you think about perspective, consider your memories. You are going to find yourself looking backward more than you want to, asking questions about why you did this or that, why you chose as you did, why this trauma happened to you, of all people.

You need the perspective of the long look at your experiences, at your motivations, at the strands of meaning that have persisted all through your life.

You need to be able to get hold of the many good parts of your married life. Your children need positive memories. All of you need the cohesive force of being able to hold to yourself those things that have been and still are uniquely yours. You don't lose everything in a divorce. It only seems that way. In fact, you can't afford to let go of everything—you have a life to rebuild. You have a future. You are facing tomorrow and the woman you will be.

As you find a place within Christ, who holds everything together, ask him to hold you together. Ask him to help you recover those good memories you have let go of but still need. Ask him to add to your life those special qualities he sees that you need. Then ask him to make you into the woman you know you can be and the woman God knows you can be.

This process will be repeated daily, and sometimes several times a day, in its shorter forms. And you will wonder whether you are making any progress at all. Keep a journal of your aspirations and feelings, your prayers, your failings, and successes. Then you will soon be able to see that you are moving ahead.

Don't expect the feelings of desperation to leave right away. The divorce does not end the trauma. Some of the things that happen in the year or two after the divorce may be as bad as anything that occurred during the marriage.

In those bad times, when I would call out to God, asking him to do something (really, I suppose, to prove that he was there), I would often hear back some lines from a hymn:

> How firm a foundation, ye saints of the Lord,
> Is laid for your faith in His excellent word!
> What more can He say, than to you He hath said,
> To you who for refuge to Jesus have fled?
> "Fear not, I am with thee, O be not dismayed,
> For I am thy God, and will still give thee aid;
> I'll strengthen thee, help thee, and cause thee to stand,
> Upheld by my righteous, omnipotent hand."

How Firm a Foundation

❦ Primary Losses

Inventory your losses, how you feel about them, and what you now need to take their place.

Losses	Feelings	Needs
1. Loss of Place		
2. Loss of Purpose		
3. Loss of People		

CHAPTER TWO

Nobody But Yourself

to be nobody but yourself—
in a world which is doing its best
night and day
to make you everybody else—
means to fight the hardest battle
which any human being can fight,
and never stop fighting.

—e.e. cummings, letter 1935

About two years after I was divorced, on a day when I
must have been feeling sorry for myself, I said, "I lost
everything in the divorce!"

My teenage son, Will, replied, "Everything except yourself, Mom." He might have added, "And except Cathy and
me and your health and your wits," and so on. But he
didn't. I hope I thanked him for his tact and for saying
exactly what I needed to hear that day.

As I thought about what Will had said to me, I remembered the e.e. cummings poem quoted above. I knew the
poem was true. And yet when it came to my time of greatest need, it seemed that hardly anyone cared about the

nobody-but-Carole person. What they seemed most interested in was role fulfillment. The public Carole who related to others in polite and predictable ways.

It may seem almost more trouble than it is worth to insist on the nobody-but-yourself part of you. It also may be that you don't know that part of yourself well enough, that you have defined yourself largely by the roles you have fulfilled. If this is the case, you need to get better acquainted with yourself, so that you will know what you have to work with.

This inner part of you—that very personal part of you that is unique, unlike anyone else—will be your primary resource in the years to come. But that inner self is now so badly bruised that it wants to give up. Don't give up. You are going to have to be your main ally, counselor, sympathizer, strategist, and so much more. You need that nobody-but-yourself. What you can accomplish in the coming years depends very much on your way of thinking and feeling, on your motivations and intentions, on your perseverance and endurance level, on your values and faith, and on your sense of humor.

"Not much of a resource!" you say. You're wrong. You are much more than you think and feel right now.

When I was in high school, I clipped a quote from *Seventeen* magazine and put it up in my room. I have thought of it occasionally in recent years because it has as much application to the woman who is divorced as it does to a teenager:

Never look down on anything about yourself.
Anything.
For although you are not now
   everything you want to be,
someday you will be all that and much more.
Value yourself now for what you can be.

But Who Are You Now?

You *were* known as a Mrs., as someone's wife. Now you feel like half a person. Your identity in your church was based partly (perhaps mainly) on your position as your husband's wife. You were known at your children's schools as a couple. You went to plays or games or concerts together. You visited other couples together.

Now who are you? Not a wife. Not part of a couple. There is no one to lean on anymore. No one to go places with, in the comfortable manner of spouses. No adult who daily cares about you.

And who are you to your children?

In the early stages of divorce, the separation is not only between Mom and Dad. The children also feel separated from their parents. Some children lose partial confidence in both parents until they can decide for themselves what is really happening and who can be believed. And the more you concealed the problems in the marriage, the more difficult it may be for your children in the first year after the divorce. If your children feel anger toward you (and they probably will), you cannot pretend that things are the same between you and them.

Who are you to people outside the home? If you have moved, you don't have the same neighbors anymore. If you have begun or changed employment, you are new again. If your church now seems an inhospitable place, you may tend to isolate yourself or look for a new church.

Just who are you? A fallen woman? A failure? I had to ask myself these questions when a disintegrating marriage was ruining every other part of life. So I looked back on my life before the marriage, to the time that God created me as a person. I had to realize that he did not create me as a wife.

Person preceded wife. And maybe only an older woman can understand that this simple fact was not at first obvious.

17

Before the 1960s, what else was there to life for most girls? What were girls raised for?

Sure, we knew that we weren't *really* created wives, but we figured God had it all planned out from way back, so that it amounted to nearly the same thing. We grew up thinking that if we were "good Christian girls" who found "nice Christian boys" to marry, everything would be okay.

Oh, it wasn't said that blatantly, but it was communicated in practical ways. We were given little preparation for marriage, almost no training in decision-making, and few other viable options in life. We were not encouraged to be honest about problems in marriage, and we were offered little help after the marriage, when serious problems arose and help was sought. We were told that women had to submit to anything their husbands wanted.

Fortunately, not too many Christian husbands in years past took extreme advantage of this privilege. Today things are different. We see behavior that is extreme and that generally comes to light only after it is fully out of control. And the church has been largely helpless to cope with the unholy wars going on in so many families.

But where does all this leave those of us who grew up in one world and now live in another? We feel as if we entered a game that was played a certain way and then someone changed the rules.

I thought back to the time and setting in which I grew up. People were much less introspective then. I didn't think much about who I was or about self-discovery. I did know that the values of nearly everything in my world were judged by men.

Women used things, but men determined values. This is not to say that every home was tyrannical or unhappy. But men were the standard of almost everything, whether or not they were experts in a subject. And most women went along with this pattern.

I grew up in a time of both social change and acquiescence. Women were no longer financially essential to the operation of the home. They had gone through two crises—depression and war—and they had survived. My friends and I watched our mothers rest in the shadows of their protectors. It was a nice life in many ways, but it was a life that changed in midstream for many of our mothers as they began working in part-time jobs outside the home in the years following World War II.

During my childhood, I got points for being good and for being smart. When divorce threatened me, I found that I couldn't look both good and smart, and I would have to choose. I chose for smart, figuring that probably I also would look good in the long run. That it turned out more or less that way didn't lessen the risk factor at the time, for I had been living in the tradition of the mothers, and now I had to get my brain in gear and solve some problems fast.

I was forced into being my most essential and real self, a self somewhat in disrepair for lack of use during the time I was playing at being the glue that held a disintegrating home together.

Who are you? You are whatever you most were many years ago. Your selfhood hasn't changed. God hasn't stopped loving you. You are who you were. You are also who you see yourself most ideally becoming. And you can walk with God into a new day and a new way of life.

To him who is able to keep you from falling and to present you before his glorious presence without fault and with great joy—to the only God our Savior be glory, majesty, power and authority, through Jesus Christ our Lord, before all ages, now and forevermore! Amen.

—Jude 24-25

What Do You Need?

What you need now is a massive dose of hope. You need a strong sense of the future. It was the Spanish philosopher Ortega y Gasset who wrote of living now in relation to the future: "Life is what comes next, what has not yet come to pass."

While I would not deny the importance of living each moment, I know that we live our moments now with an eye to the future. Today's ideals and failures touch tomorrow.

When life is structured and in order, you don't have to think constantly about the future just to accomplish relatively simple tasks. But when life is in disarray and confusion, when you have suffered severe loss and change, when the structures have been knocked down, you need consciously to plot out even the simplest moves just to get from here to there.

You need to be kind to yourself and give yourself the benefit of the doubt whenever possible. You need faith in yourself. You are at a very low point right now, but the entire experience can make you so strong that in the coming years you will far surpass any goals you set today.

This poem by Emily Dickinson speaks of what we can do if we don't keep pulling ourselves down:

We never know how high we are, till we are called
   to rise,

And then if we are true to form, our statures touch
  the skies.
The heroism we recite would be a daily thing,
Did not ourselves the cubits warp, for fear to be a king.

You also need the common sense and realism to be able to judge things as they truly are. You don't want unrealistic evaluations or false hopes. Your larger success in these next years depends on small successes along the way. And you don't want to chalk up a string of failures that come from bad planning.

If you don't have a career already in gear, it might be wise to have some testing done, possibly at a local community college or career guidance office.

If you are at a loss to know where to start with your finances, seek some help. In fact, get two opinions from people who deal with business and finance every day, a banker or a businessperson, for example. Read newspapers and business magazines. Also, there are some excellent books on the market for single parents. While you probably won't become a financial wizard, you will pick up the rudiments of personal finance.

Money is something you will think about often in relation to many parts of your life. Unfortunately, money—or the lack of it—is one of the greatest producers of pressure, frustration, and injustice for many divorced women and their children.

The quiet heroism I have seen and heard of in many single parents, the day-and-night work they do just to keep bread on the table and also be parents, says volumes about human potential. Along with a full work schedule, they are picking up the parenting that was shared before, planning special times for the children, and trying to reestablish some level of normality in the home. And knowing from experience the financial nightmare that so many of them face, the constant lack that runs routine matters into major crises, I respect the motivation of love that keeps them on this path of faithfulness.

Because they have survived and because I have, I know that you can too.

I do know that I could not have survived those years without the grace and provision of the Lord. I guess I was bartering with the Lord at times—"I'll do my part, but you had better come through and take up all the slack." I don't regret that, since this type of bartering has a long history, right back to some of the Old Testament patriarchs. And God worked with it or around it, however he sees those dimensions. The important thing is that he never disregards the desperation or extremity of people who call on him in time of need. He is a God of mercy and kindness, and he loves you better than you love yourself right now. And he loves your children and will not forsake them.

Great is Thy faithfulness,
O God my Father,
There is no shadow of turning with Thee;
Thou changest not,
Thy compassions they fail not;
As Thou hast been Thou forever wilt be.
Great is Thy faithfulness!
Great is Thy faithfulness!
Morning by morning new mercies I see.
All I have needed Thy hand hath provided—
Great is Thy faithfulness, Lord unto me.

Great Is Thy Faithfulness

Setting Goals

To facilitate the recovery that you want to happen, it is important for you to set goals. In the charts at the end of this chapter, you will see that I have broken the goal-setting into time periods: five years, two years, one year, and three months. I know that you can't accurately project five-year goals now. The exactness doesn't matter. What does matter is that you set yourself in a direction with a sense of right-ness about it.

You obviously have far more control over three-month goals than over a one-year goal. But if your ambition is to finish school, you need to plan a year ahead, two years ahead, or you won't make it.

The three-month segments and one-year goals should fit inside the longer time periods. Your objectives for three months should be smaller, less ambitious, and far more specific than those for two years.

To break goals down into day-to-day details, have a special place (bulletin board, a calendar, a "to-do" pad) where you can note items you especially need to work on today or this week. I suggest that alongside your goals you list your thanks for successes and blessings.

The benefit of keeping a record is that you very soon begin to see progress and change. To have a record of that progress is vital, since most of us are marvelous forgetters. As you see and remind yourself of change in the matters you are most concerned about, you can know that you are beginning to leave your problems behind you. When the children and I moved into our new home, I bought a Nothing Book in which to record what would happen to us, in us, and for us in the years to come. My book began in October of 1978. At the beginning of each three months, I wrote down my goals for that time. My goals were mostly prayers, written in the presence of God. Then I had a couple of pages on which I recorded the main events of the three months, not all at once, but every few weeks, as I thought of something.

Looking back through my book reminded me of the variety I knew was there—goals about job, money, needs of my children, my inner struggles, the need for friends, items relating to church, decorating, car, losing some pounds, and so on. Within the first year, my lists were long. Looking back to the period of April-June 1979, I saw these items:

Goals

1. Get contract for P.J. book (for which I was co-author)
2. Friends, personal closeness
3. Summer plans for children
4. Get a raise, move into author acquisitions
5. A greater ease and maturity
6. A sense of expectancy and joy
7. Organize closets better
8. Have work done on car
9. Greater realism, self-understanding
10. Will's schoolwork
11. Live more quietly, more richly
12. Allow no victimization of me
13. Know God in a more personal way
14. Trust God to give me his goals for my life

Events

1. Received contract for P.J. book
2. Rented cottage for a week in Wisconsin
3. Trip to see Cathy at Easter time
4. Am moving more into acquisitions
5. More energy, more acceptance of my life

6. Repairs done on car
7. Thanks for the recovery in this year
8. Cathy home from school, a successful year
9. Jeanann's shower here
10. Trip to Daisy's conference
11. Deep sense of the Holy Spirit's presence
12. Heightened sense of my value and capabilities
13. Meeting T.C.

Not all of the entries are this positive, of course. In fact, I also read poignant pleas to God for healing and guidance. I read of my old feelings of helplessness. But the primary impression as I read back through the years noted in my book is that we have been stabilized, settled. Life is much easier now than it was.

This stabilization is not a surprise, for it is just what is promised to Christians going through a hard time: "The God of all grace, who called you to his eternal glory in Christ, after you have suffered a little while, will himself restore you and make you strong, firm and steadfast" (1 Peter 5:10).

Reasons for Planning

I think of four major reasons for setting goals and staying with them.

Widening your scope
If you plot long-range goals, you are more likely to give attention to a wider scope of your life than if you just approach things at random or deal with the most urgent crisis.

When a woman deals only in the short-range or goes from one crisis to another, it is easy for her to skip those challenges that seem difficult. She could say with Scarlett O'Hara, "I'll think about that tomorrow." And with the schedule and emotional turmoil most divorced women have, tomorrow never comes.

Envisioning yourself

It is important to be able to envision yourself as a unity, not as a fragmented person. Made as you are in the image of God, you reflect the unity of God himself. God, of course, does not find his center in another, but people do. And the only adequate center for a person is God.

When the apostle Peter wrote about the quiet inner beauty of women, he spoke primarily of married women and the way they were to be submissive to their husbands. Even so, I think he was writing of a characteristic common to all women. He asked that they not consider their main attraction to be beautiful clothing or jewels but the hidden beauty "of your inner self, the unfading beauty of a gentle and quiet spirit, which is of great worth in God's sight. For this is the way the holy women of the past who put their hope in God used to make themselves beautiful. They were submissive to their own husbands" (1 Peter 3:4-5).

It is from this quiet center, this hidden inner self, that a woman responds properly to her husband. But it is also from this inner self that any woman must live. That inside place feels particularly empty right now, and your natural impulse will be to pursue substitutes for your husband or to take up a frantic pace of activity.

The frenetic schedule will do little to satisfy and will go a long way toward destroying the very quietness that you need. If you want a quiet spirit, you will have to pursue it consciously, keeping it in mind as you restructure your life. For there is nothing that you need more right now than this quiet center of beauty and tranquility.

Because you will have a more-than-full day, you may find that the only time free for reflection, prayer, and Bible reading is early morning. While you may think that an extra bit of sleep will help you more, I think you will find in the long run that getting up earlier and spending the time with the Lord without interruption will do more than anything else to bring you to the unity of person you so much need.

The LORD your God is with you,
he is mighty to save.
He will take great delight in you,
he will quiet you with his love,
he will rejoice over you with singing.

—Zephaniah 3:17

Facing the future

Beyond the more immediate benefits of planning, there is another far-reaching and basic reason for setting goals. The Christian is always faced toward the future. We live today in hope of our eternal future with God. We live today looking forward to the last day, which is the first day. And we know that all things on earth are tentative; we are just passing through.

You are part of a long story that is going to end-begin with the greatest beauty, excitement, and joy. And you will be part of the story then too, for you will live in the prepared city in the presence of the King. You can read about this in Revelation 21–22.

I am not suggesting that eternal hope or relationship with God takes the place of human relationships, but it does put our earthly life into perspective. It tells us that the end of the story has to be part of the beginning.

For a Christian not to plan, not to have a high sense of becoming and changing, is a contradiction. We are to be changed, day by day, until we stand in God's presence.

When the apostle John was an old man, he knew that he would soon be with Christ. And he wrote to the Christians of his day: "Dear friends, now we are children of God, and what we will be has not yet been made known. But we know that when he appears, we shall be like him, for we shall see him as he is. Everyone who has this hope in him purifies himself, just as he is pure" (1 John 3:2-3).

With faith in the unseen city—whose maker and builder is God—with hope in the One who has secured your place in that city, and with love for those who travel with you, you can make it, not only to the other side but also to tomorrow.

And on that day when you see Jesus as he is, you will for the first time look in a mirror that is clear, not hazy, and you will see that you look like Jesus. For the essence of completeness is to be like the center.

In this transitional time in your life, when everything seems up for grabs, give that everything into his hands and let him hold you together—a woman becoming complete.

Feeling significant

You need to feel significant. But before you can, you need to be convinced that what you are now doing is important. To my knowledge, very few people have ever stated that recovering from divorce, doing the many remedial things that are part of this, is important. Quite the opposite. The process is generally regarded as life in the leper colony, the mop-up of failure.

Because you will encounter such attitudes and several more that aren't especially inspiring, let it be said right now that what you do and become in the next months and years is *very* important. For you and for your children. For other women going through the same tragedy. For your parents and other family members who are suffering with you.

The very process of setting goals will jar you out of lethargy, self-pity, and selfish indulgence on days when you want to give up and say it just doesn't make any difference. That you don't matter.

Setting goals will remind you of the potential for all you can be and for all you do in the years to come. The hazy outlines of the future that you see when you dream and plan will give shape to small specific things you do today and tomorrow. And those outlines will become beacons far down the road, having great drawing power, as more and more you see the possibilities that are even now beginning to take shape.

❧ Goal Setting

Decide where you are now and where you'd like to be three months, one year, two years from now.

	Now	Three Months	One Year	Two Years
1. My feelings about myself				
2. My feelings about my ex-spouse				
3. My job				
4. Money				
5. Our home				

6. Church

7. Friends

8. Emotional
   stability

9. Spiritual growth

10.

11.

12.

	Now	Three Months	One Year	Two Years
Child 1:				
Child 2:				
Child 3:				

Actions to take
(write the date)

1.

2.

3.

You Are Forgivable

He alone can make forgiveness
something glorious to remember.

—Louis Evely

I will turn their mourning into
gladness . . . and give them joy to
outdo their sorrow.

—Jeremiah 31:13, NEB

Y ou are redeemable. You can create a truly good life.
You can give your children roots again. You can be
accepted.

You are lovable. Most people may not be demonstrating
that right now, and you may not feel very lovable. You have
been involved in wrong and embarrassment. Even if no
one has criticized your behavior, you are part of a marriage
that foundered.

It could be that your primary fault in the marriage was in
permitting certain wrongs to go on, in not blowing the
whistle, because you were convinced that it was your wife-

ly duty to be quietly loyal, to submit to anything you could tolerate.

Or maybe you were the partner more at fault. It may be that what people are thinking and saying about you is true.

Whatever the situation, I hope you will not feel the need forever to explain and hang dirty wash all over town. If you were obviously more at fault than your ex-husband (however such things are judged), it is more likely that someone will come to you about your need of forgiveness. If, on the other hand, you are generally judged to be the innocent party, it is unlikely that people will speak to you about forgiveness, for they won't think that you have done anything that requires it.

Even if you sincerely feel that you did everything in your power to make the marriage what it should have been, you still know your need of forgiveness. No one has to tell you that you need restoration, not only to God but also to yourself and other people. But unless someone brings it to your attention, you probably won't pursue it. You have so much else to do, and most of the people through whom forgiveness should be mediated aren't being overly cordial to you.

Forgiveness and Grief

I almost stumbled on forgiveness. Having gone through some terrible weeks of feeling that I was in a pit, not really knowing what I needed, I went one last time to Earl, the Christian psychologist my ex-husband and I had talked with for six months. His response to me was, "You have obviously been grieving; you need to work all the way through it."

Grieving is as necessary in divorce as it is in a time of death. In fact, we may lose more through divorce than we lose when a spouse dies. Certainly there are more feelings of stress and guilt and confusion.

When your life seems clouded, when all else is obliterated except your loss, when you can't seem to think clearly about much of anything except the darkness around you and the lack of light ahead—don't fight it. You can't bottle up your sorrow. You can't afford to ignore it. Find help from a caring person who understands grief. There is nothing wrong with grieving the loss of marriage and husband and the place you have had in life. There would be something wrong with you if you did not grieve.

After Earl had helped me identify my grief and after I had begun to come out of it, my son began grieving. And then it hit my daughter. I was so glad it had come to me first, so that I could help them through this dark and painful place.

After Earl and I had talked about the grieving process, I asked his theological opinion about my actions in filing for divorce. At least I thought I was asking a theological question. But he knew what I needed, and with great tenderness he assured me that God knows when we are in impossible situations and that he understands. I went back to my office and said to a friend, "I feel freed. Absolved. Forgiven."

God was forgiving all the time, but it took a word from one of his servants to assure me of it. Intellectually, I knew that God understood. What I needed was assurance that he was feeling what I felt and that he would still love me. I needed to *hear* that assurance because I was feeling such condemnation from so many people in the church.

To be effectual, forgiveness needs the touch of those within the body of Christ. It is not enough for church members merely to encourage the divorced person to go to God and ask for forgiveness. The people in the body need to demonstrate God's forgiveness by expressing their own forgiveness of the divorced person. If that is not happening, if there are cuts and tears, the kind of forgiveness God promised is not taking place.

I know all too well what part of the problem is—good church people don't want to appear to condone divorce. Soon after my divorce, a relative of my former husband assured me of his family's love and interest. Then he added, "But we don't believe in divorce." To which I quickly responded, "And do you think I do?"

Forgiveness and the Church

The church's lack of attention to the matter of forgiveness is evidenced by the very low level of church attendance among newly divorced people who normally go to church and by the fact that so many divorced people change churches. It is also evidenced by the lack of recovery and growth in many divorced people. If we listen to statistics, we hear that many church-going divorced people are sexually promiscuous. Such sexual activity outside of marriage is just not part of life for a person living in God's grace and forgiveness. And while there is no excuse for the behavior, there is a way to explain it, relating to the lack in the church. The church needs to recognize that this behavior may be in part due to its own absence of healthy involvement with the divorced person.

A person who has failed—who feels soiled and used and victimized and who has no help to get out of that mire—may decide that she has no choice but to go on feeling that way. While this attitude indicates little understanding of biblical teaching about forgiveness, it does accurately represent segments of the church that have given low emphasis to forgiveness.

For the Christian, forgiveness is not an option but a necessity. Forgiveness is needed for all sins, not just for the shredding of a marriage. People who lie need forgiveness, as do people who cheat God out of their energy and money. People who are brutal and angry need forgiveness. Everyone does—and yet somehow, much of the church has avoided this.

When you have come to the point where you can no longer hide your troubles, you are at your lowest. But if you choose to look at it in another light, you can believe that you are on the way up. Even if you make that choice, you may be a scandal, an embarrassment to other people. You cause confusion.

The main complication in reaching for forgiveness in community is that many people will be indifferent to you. Or they may condemn you or be afraid of you. When there always seems to be forty feet between you and the people you know, you get tired of trying to bridge the distance. But other people's wrong attitudes do not provide you an adequate excuse to evade what you need to do.

As I was writing this chapter, I visited a church in our town and saw a unique demonstration of public forgiveness. The pastor went to the pulpit and read the story of the prodigal son and the father who ran out to embrace his wayward son. Then the pastor said, "There is someone with us this morning who has not been here for quite a while. Many of us have been concerned and have prayed for him. Today we want him to know that we are glad he is back."

Then the pastor named the man and asked him to come to the front of the church. As the man came, the pastor went down near the communion table to meet him and to enclose him in the embrace of reconciliation, in the name of the congregation. Members were urged to greet him after the service and offer their encouragement.

The man's failing and absence were public knowledge. How fitting, then, that his return should also be public, as a seal on the forgiveness that had obviously already been sought and received. This pictured so well the horizontal element of forgiveness.

While I am not suggesting this form for divorced people, something needs to be done, in public as well as in private, to make sure that forgiveness is not only sought and received, but also believed, by the divorced person and by the congregation. I know of one pastor who at times serves communion privately to a person in need of the healing touch of forgiveness. He also may pronounce an absolution from the guilt that divorced people often can't let go of.

Forgiveness and Family Patterns

You may feel some guilt for another reason that is difficult to understand at times, for it involves wrongs that you had nothing to do with. Families live in patterns and those patterns of behavior repeat themselves in one generation after another and become joined to other patterns. When you are part of a family system, the behaviors can become so automatic that you don't even notice the ways you and your relatives are interacting with each other.

We hear much today about dysfunctional families; in fact we even hear statements about all families being dysfunctional in some ways. I think that is overstating the case, because there are many families who maintain loving and supportive relationships and who confront difficulties together and solve problems effectively. Yet, even within these families, there can be behaviors that are harmful and that go almost unnoticed—or are denied—for year after year, until . . . until a tragedy occurs.

You have just gone through a tragedy and you may be looking at your family, and that of your former spouse, in ways that you never have before. You may be seeing twisted motives, harsh behaviors, unrealistic expectations, private rebellions, unpredictable responses, as well as un-spoken assumptions that are understood by all and that create pressures to conform to what the family expects.

While you are not responsible for these behaviors and attitudes, you are responsible for the way you now react to them. You and your children do not need additional weights on you as you approach a future in which so much has changed.

As you study your families, you will probably find much that is good and much that is neither good nor bad. But you will undoubtedly discover some behaviors that need to be changed, at least as they relate to you and your children. This is where you enter in, because you are the only one who can effect this kind of change.

For me, the first step was recognizing what needed to be changed. The second step involved forgiveness of traits in our families, some of them lasting for generations, that needed the liberating power that only God can give. I didn't want my children to be prisoners to old hurts, and so I asked God to forgive those wrongs of the past and then to break their power in our lives. I thought so often of the two lines of Charles Wesley's hymn:

> He breaks the power of canceled sin,
> He sets the prisoner free.

The third step took much longer, as I had to set about structuring minor changes here and there, not rejecting family members, but at times letting this or that one know that we were not going to be involved in certain behaviors or reactions or assumptions anymore. We will talk more about this in Chapter 5.

If you are part of a family in which there is serious dysfunction, you may need to take more drastic action to remove yourself and your children from behaviors that are harmful. Do not hesitate to do what is necessary. You are responsible for the emotional and spiritual and physical health of your family, and this may call for great courage on your part to do what is needed.

Forgiveness and Money

One of your pressing needs is money. The living standard of most divorced mothers goes down, way down. Also, many of them have not been employed in jobs that could support the family.

You may be watching your former spouse enjoy a considerable rise in income as yours goes down. You need to be sure your children are provided for, and part of this provision probably includes child support from their father. Know in detail what is spelled· out in the divorce decree, and do your best to receive what you should. Most decrees stipulate that fathers should pay for large medical and dental expenses, as well as regular support.

In the past, so many fathers have been remiss in paying child support that there are now laws governing payment in many states. Child support is not optional. It is something to which the custodial parent is entitled. Fathers are obliged to support their children, and you are not a bad woman if, failing to receive that support, you go after it.

I know there is considerable disagreement about the matter of taking legal action against a person who will not fulfill his obligations. As I was writing this chapter, my pastor preached a sermon on forgiveness as part of a series on the Lord's Prayer. I wondered what he would think about what I was advising in this section. And so I called him to ask whether he thought forgiveness meant that a woman who was unable to obtain the money for her children from her former husband should just take the loss. His reply was, "Absolutely not. She is doing him a favor in forcing him to meet his obligations."

I appreciated his response because it confirmed what I have long felt to be the biblical position on this. Paul's word to Timothy is plain, "If anyone does not provide for his relatives, and especially for his immediate family, he has denied the faith and is worse than an unbeliever" (1 Timothy 5:8).

In 1 Corinthians 6, Paul urged that the church should sit as a court over disputes rather than leaving Christians no alternative but to go to court. This seems to be in concord with Jesus' advice in Matthew 18 about dealing with such problems. Unfortunately, most people who seek help from the church run into a stone wall and are left with two alternatives—going to court or taking the loss. For a woman trying to provide for her children on a reduced income, taking the loss is just not an acceptable solution.

Forgiveness and Excusing

Part of understanding forgiveness is knowing the difference between forgiving and excusing. You can have a forgiving attitude and still insist that other people meet their obligations. You didn't agree to those obligations; they did. It is their responsibility to see that they meet them.

This distinction between forgiving and excusing is crucial when someone has done you or your children a serious wrong and then refuses to acknowledge the wrong. There are many offenders today who create havoc for years and then try to blame their sins on other people. One woman who had been molested by her father for ten years of her childhood told me that he later wrote her a letter forgiving her for the wrong she had done against him! He was totally unwilling—or unable—to see his own wrongdoing.

For this woman, and for others in like situations, there is no normal means of dealing with forgiveness—if normal means forgiving when the other person acknowledges his wrong.

In such cases forgiveness may have to be worked out in an appropriate way between you and God. You do not want to be consumed with anger, and if your thoughts return again and again to the occasion of wrong and the perpetrator, you know that you have not resolved the issue. Obviously, you cannot excuse the wrong in saying that whatever happened doesn't matter. And, you can forgive the person in your heart and work out that forgiveness in your behavior. But you may still have to deal with the consequences of the wrong. Be sure that you don't deny the results of sins against you or your children.

One outcome of unresolved anger is bitterness. The writer of the Book of Hebrews spoke of this bitterness when he said, "Make every effort to live in peace with all men and to be holy; without holiness no one will see the Lord. See to it that no one misses the grace of God and that no bitter root grows up to cause trouble and defile many" (Hebrews 12:14-15).

Your family doesn't need any bitter roots or bitter fruit. Ask God for wisdom to understand about the anger you feel. And then ask him to help you in resolving it in appropriate and helpful ways. If you cannot do this alone, don't hesitate to seek guidance from a spiritual advisor.

Forgiveness and Your Future

One reason forgiveness is so essential for you is that you have a future. You will not be able to walk into the kind of future God has in mind for you if you do not first experience this sense of wrongs made right, of burdens lifted, of dirty places cleansed, of the unacceptable made acceptable. You will not find real fellowship anywhere in the church until you can know that you have crossed this bridge. Nor will you feel the necessary confidence to help your children into their future.

If you have walked with God in the past, have known forgiveness from sins, and are aware of the indwelling Holy Spirit, you know that a different standard is in operation for you than for the non-Christian. You need to see yourself once again as the loved child of the heavenly Father. You need the comfort, guidance, and teaching of the compassionate Holy Spirit. You need to be reminded that you have been redeemed at great price by the suffering and risen Savior.

A deep experience of the grace of God during and after a divorce will become a stabilizing factor for you. Your life has been harsh, ugly, mean, tearing, and nightmarish in recent times—anything but an experience of grace. You can rest in the grace of God, feel his drawing and caring love, know his concern for your children, and hear his voice of encouragement.

Because of the LORD's great love we are not consumed,
for his compassions never fail.
They are new every morning;
great is your faithfulness.

—Lamentations 3:22-23

If you know yourself to be graced, to be favored, to be cared for by a loving heavenly Father, for even one beautiful moment, you have reason to know that you will soon be able to get beyond the feelings that are ugly and mean and awful. They just aren't appropriate around such grace.

God is at work in you, not necessarily doing anything now about the hopeless situation, but rather moving you ever closer to the good. In the Spanish Bible, Romans 8:28

has the sense of urging the person toward the good. And the ultimate good is God. "And we know that to those who love God, all things help them to the good, those, that is, who are called to conform to His will" *(Antigua Version de Casiodoro de Reina,* 1569).

As you begin to be more aware of God's presence, you will see in a growing way the continuity of his work in you. You will be reassured that God loves people who cry, people who fail, people who sin, as well as people who are smilingly succeeding at the moment.

Christ spoke about worship and the filling of the Holy Spirit to a woman who was a five-time loser at marriage. And he gave her—the Samaritan woman with a live-in lover—the privilege of being a missionary. He knew the facts of her life would change, just as her heart had changed in that moment of realizing his forgiving love (John 4).

Christ protected the woman about to be stoned for her sin, by reminding the people that they all had equal need of forgiveness (John 8).

Christ quietly allowed a woman to anoint his feet with perfume and then dry them with her hair. In this moving scene, he let a woman who had sinned much and who had found forgiveness minister to him (Luke 7:36-50).

God through Christ is reconciling the world to himself. And this reconciliation is for all people and all kinds of failings. But it is usually made effective through someone who understands the need for forgiveness and second chances.

In his book *Release from Phoniness,* Arnold Prater tells the story of a young British doctor who had to perform an emergency tracheotomy on a six-year-old boy. Since the doctor had never performed the operation before, he felt great trepidation during the surgery. And he wasn't very encouraged by his assistant who was a young nurse just out of training. But the surgery was successful, and the doctor told the nurse to stay with the boy through the night to make sure that the tube into the windpipe stayed open, so that the boy could breathe.

Early the next morning, the doctor heard a knock at his door. It was the young nurse. Exhausted from the stress of the surgery, she had fallen asleep—and the boy had died.

The doctor lost his head and swore that she would have to pay for this and that he would certainly see that she was reported. After a while he called her into his office and read the report to her while she stood there trembling with fear and overcome with remorse and shame. When he had finished he said, "Well, have you anything to say?" She fearfully nodded her head and dared to look up and turn her tear-splashed face toward him. "Please, sir," she said falteringly, "give me another chance."

It had not occurred to the doctor that he might do this. It was all cut and dried so far as he was concerned. She had failed. Her mistake had cost a life. She must pay. It was just that simple.

But that night he could not sleep. He kept hearing her cry, "Please give me another chance." All night he wrestled with reminders of mercy and compassion. The next morning he tore up the report.

Years later the young nurse went on to become head of a great children's hospital, loved by all, giving herself over and over again to children who needed her love and great heart. Suppose the girl had fled and not faced up to the wrong that was in her actions? Suppose the good doctor had not given her another chance? Ah, but that is idle speculation—for he did!

Well, would God do any less than he? The good doctor would be the first to deny this. He is a God of the second chance. That is why He exchanges prodigals' rags for purple robes of royalty. Because He is a God of beginning again.[1]

One of your most profound needs right now is an abiding assurance of forgiveness. Please don't ignore this necessary element in your recovery, in your beginning again.

I am well aware that some members of the clergy are not prepared to deal with forgiveness for the divorced person. If this is so in your church, pray that the Lord will lead you to someone who can understand and help you toward what you need from God and from at least some of his people.

He giveth more grace when the burdens grow greater,
He sendeth more strength when the labors increase;
To added affliction He addeth His mercy,
To multiplied trials, His multiplied peace.

When we have exhausted our store of endurance,
When our strength has failed ere the day is half done,
When we reach the end of our hoarded resources,
Our Father's full giving is only begun.

His love has no limit, His grace has no measure,
His power has no boundary known unto men;
For out of His infinite riches in Jesus,
He giveth and giveth and giveth again.

—*Annie Johnson Flint*

❦ Wrongs That Need to Be Forgiven

List some of the actions and attitudes that need forgiveness.

My actions:

_____

_____

_____

_____

My former spouse's actions:

_____

_____

_____

_____

Learned and inherited traits and behaviors:

_____

_____

_____

_____

Friends and relatives:

_____

_____

_____

_____

CHAPTER FOUR

At Home in Your Home

The most excellent end for which we
are created is that one should teach
another about God, what He is in His
being, what His will is, how He is
minded towards us.

—Martin Luther

We are not primarily put on this earth
to see through one another, but to see
one another through.

—Peter De Vries

H ome. The word has hundreds of meanings for each
of us. Home is sights and sounds and smells and
shared experiences. Home is how it was when we were
children of five or nine or thirteen. Home is the specialness
we felt on holidays when the relatives came. Home is all
the days when nothing unusual happened and the few
days when together we suffered the trauma of illnesses or
death or separation.

Home is the place we left for new ventures and then came back to. Home is the people we have lived with, mostly relatives, but some others along the way too.

After you married, home was a new house or apartment and babies and working together through some tough problems and knowing you and your husband could make it. Home was the place where your friends came. It was those first nights with a frightened puppy or kitten. Home felt so good after a vacation.

And at the very center of your home was the bond—however tenuous—between you and your husband, the promise of security, growth and love that you felt together. That is, until things went wrong. And because that bond was so central, home just isn't the same for you anymore.

In Par Lagerkvist's story, "The Marriage Feast," Jonas Samuelson and Frida Johansson are about to be married in a small ceremony in her home. Neither is young any longer, and they have accommodated themselves to the quietness of life alone—when suddenly the wonder of a growing love comes to them.

As Frida is preparing to go downstairs to the parlor where their guests are waiting, Lagerkvist reveals her hopes:

> Oh, if only everything goes off all right, and it's the kind of festival she has hoped for, that she has dreamed about so much. If only it's all as the great solemnity of the occasion demands.
>
> What is there on earth greater than two people being made one, meeting before God to have their compact sealed at the throne of the Eternal One?
>
> Their lives were to be united, they were to be made one, their souls were to be joined together forever. Neither of them would be lonely any more, neither she nor Jonas.

The story ends that night after Frida and Jonas are asleep, their hands clasped.

And like a heavenly song of praise, like a hosanna of light around the only living thing, the stars rose around their bed in mighty hosts, their numbers increasing with the darkness.[1]

When you married, you too felt the holy wonder of what was happening. You thought that what was sealed before God's throne would be secured there also. You believed you would not be lonely again, for you too glimpsed the stars rising around you. This holy wonder was the beginning of your home.

Now there is no song of praise. No hosanna of light. The stars have fallen. The compact sealed at the throne of the Eternal One has come undone. And the Eternal One—is he perhaps not as you were led to think?

Your home is the primary place where you will be reminded day after day that the great wonder of marriage has turned to ashes. That the God who was supposed to lead you into his perfect will seems to have failed you. Home is where you will decide how to think about all this.

Feeling at Home

Some divorced and widowed women just won't stay home. They won't face the emptiness, the drastic change that has happened to them. So they keep on the run, using the house as a place to sleep and change clothes. This running may go on for years, but eventually it has to stop if they are ever to have a normal and productive life.

Decide right from the beginning not to run away from the realities that surround you. If you have more than you can face right now, your subconscious will shield you from dealing with all of them at once and will let you space them to your tolerance level. Determine to deal with the changes as honestly and effectively as you can.

Most of your resource to do this is inside yourself. Yet looking squarely inside yourself may be the most difficult of all. You aren't at your best, to put it mildly. You look in the mirror and don't like what you see. You listen to your tone of voice and don't like what you hear. You feel how shaky you are in relatively simple situations and wonder if you will ever again be whole. You watch yourself overreact to little events and despair that the woman you thought was so mature has come to this.

You are thrust into the role of wage earner and sole parent in the home, and you may be ill-equipped to manage either one. In your marriage, you may have been far too dependent on your husband. Now you feel like a defenseless waif in a harsh, cold world, and you want to cry and rage at the same time.

The Quakers practice a method of finding quietness in the midst of turmoil. They call it centering. In your pain you can center down into yourself and insist on times of deep quiet in which you surrender your inner self to God. The contemplatives of the Middle Ages called this *recollection*. It is a time to become still, to enter a recreating silence, to let the fragmentation of your mind be centered on God.[2] This may seem incongruous to your life demands and to the conflict you have passed through. And you may find yourself running from the quiet and from what you will find deep inside you.

The pursuit of quietness receives its motivation not from the frenetic society around you but from God himself. And its result is a greater knowledge of him and an appreciation of the value of your inner self made in his likeness.

As you quietly recollect, you will begin to see yourself and your situation differently. For instance, you may be feeling pressured because you have to live more simply than you want to. But you could look at it this way: you now have the unique opportunity to live with greater simplicity than you have been able to for a long time. Life became cluttered with so many obligations and things and tensions and angers and unresolved problems. Now you can shed much of the mental and emotional baggage you have been carrying around. You can learn the beauty of quietness as you listen for the sounds of silence. For silence does have its own language.

You can insist on looking deep inside yourself in the presence of God, letting him show you yourself, little by little, as he sees you are ready. For he alone fully understands your motivations, tensions, and past problems. He alone sees all the pressures that bear upon you. He alone knows your breaking point. And as you trust your inner self into his hands, you will be safe in his love. And you can know that he will honor your trust and will work in the cocoon of the quiet place you have made in your home, to insure that the butterfly is perfectly formed.

You can't do this kind of quiet work around other people. It isn't a public thing. You do this at home. And as you do, you will make your home more truly yours because you are insisting that soul work be done there on a regular basis.

Have mercy on me, O God, have mercy on me,
for in you my soul takes refuge.
I will take refuge in the shadow of your wings
until the disaster has passed.

I cry out to God Most High,
to God, who fulfills his purpose for me.
He sends from heaven and saves me,
rebuking those who hotly pursue me;
God sends his love and his faithfulness.

—Psalm 57:1-3

In his book *The Wounded Healer*, Henri Nouwen talks about the ministry of hospitality and about your need to feel at home in *your* home. When you have known God's healing, you will want to extend his love to others.

What does hospitality as a healing power require? It requires first of all the host feel at home in his own house, and secondly that he create a free and fearless place for the unexpected visitor. . . . anyone who wants to pay attention without intention has to be at home in his own house—that is, he has to discover the center of his life in his own heart. . . . By withdrawing into ourselves, not out of self-pity but out of humility, we create the space for another to be made himself. . . . When we are not afraid to enter into our own center and to concentrate on the stirrings of our own soul, we come to know that being alive means being loved. . . . When we have found the anchor places for our lives in our own center, we can be free to let others enter into the space created for them, and allow them to dance their own dance, sing their own song and speak their own language without fear.[3]

The idea of being at home in your own house seems so obvious at first that it may take some time to realize that you don't feel all that much at home anymore. Yet, as you bring under control the details of living, as you and your children find the healing grace of God to be effective, as you truly make a home that reflects you, and as you reach out then to share your home with others, your home will become a place to treasure.

Home and Money

At home, more than any other place, you will be reminded about money. You make your money at work, but you decide how to spend it at home. Home is where the bills are. Home is where you daily see that you have come into reduced circumstances. Home is where your children ask for good things that you just can't afford.

Home is where you will fashion a new way of life, and most of your choices will involve money. It is at home that you will decide how to manage the money you do have, to make it work for you. The amount you have is not as important as its management. Even if you mentally place responsibility for your past and present money problems on your spouse, that doesn't mean that you are free now. You need to give a good deal of consideration to making your money stretch in many directions.

Home is the place where you will decide to hold on to or let go of the resentments about your former spouse and money. I know women who, even though they received large settlements, still carry bitter resentments into the years after the divorce because their lifestyle isn't the same as their ex-husband's. And the more money involved in the settlement, the more resentment there may be over what the women didn't get. I suppose that's normal, but it's still deadly. The resentments can be strong even if the amount to be divided is small. When a good friend of mine found out that my former husband had purchased a large house while the children and I were still in an apartment and with very little money, she was so angry she urged me to take him to court for more money.

Most settlements are unfair, if you listen to one side of the story. And it is sad that there has been so little help in getting fair settlements. But to carry resentment for years and years and to fill the home with bitterness just isn't intelligent. Nor is it good for your health. Yes, I have sometimes felt angry about money—and with good reason. And it has been primarily at home that I have had to work through my feelings about money.

Priorities

Managing your money means setting priorities. What matters most in your life? Assuming that you don't have time and money to do some of the things you want to do, what will you choose?

You're in a new situation—new arrangements, new forms, new combinations. The old, familiar things are replaced by the unfamiliar, the strange, the threatening. But God can pour freshness into the unwanted newness you now face.

God has special concern for the fatherless and the widows. Maybe you don't feel that you and your children fit into these categories, but there are godly people who think that you do. And even if God's people are not demonstrating the concern for you that they should, God has his own ways of seeing that women and children in special need are cared for. You will want to relate to him in an attitude of trust and expectancy, knowing that he is a loving Father who will not forsake his own. This attitude of faith will take much of the stress out of your legitimate concerns about money. It does not remove the concerns, of course, but it allows you to use your energies in channels that are productive.

Yet, if your situation is like mine, you will be confronted again and again by unexpected expenses and with no extra money to fall back on, even though you have done your best to work it all out. In those times—when you are down to nothing and an emergency happens—you can look with confidence to your heavenly Father for his supply of that need.

It is good to place some of your spending with a long view in mind. If you want to take your children on a vacation next summer, you will probably have to say no to some extras now. Or, on a lesser scale, you may like to eat out often. But if that destroys your household budget, it isn't worth it.

What are your priorities? What matters most to you and your children? What are the necessities? When you plan your money management around them, you all will be more satisfied than if you just respond to urgencies.

Prayer and money

As you consider money and priorities, don't forget about prayer. Since God is the supplier of all that you have, and since he has special concern for those in need, and because your caring Father is moved by the sadness and hurt your children have suffered, he certainly wants you to come to him with your wants and needs. No, you won't get everything you want. But you *will* learn that God's grace connects with your money in a special way.

When we first moved to our apartment, I knew that we had no money for accidents or replacement of much of anything. And I thought of the prayers offered by the children of Israel in the wilderness. You may remember that during forty years, their clothing and household items didn't wear out. I wasn't expecting forty years of use, but I prayed that we would not have accidents, that our car and clothing and household items would last, and that we would have a minimum of extra expense. That prayer was answered.

Even the apartment we lived in was a provision from the Lord. In 1978, when I knew we would be needing housing, my mother heard that a mission was constructing an apartment building in our area. I contacted the manager who held the apartment for me for six months. It was everything we needed—three bedrooms, two baths, large rooms, a clean, quiet, secure place, and with rent lower than we would have paid anywhere else.

I experienced this same provision for a job. In early 1978, I was working part-time and had already told the personnel manager that if I went full-time, I would like to be in the book division. When I was sure that I would need full-time employment, one of the book editors "happened" to leave to go back to school. Within a few weeks, both housing and job were supplied.

I prayed that God would show me how to reduce our living expenses. Within just a few days, I discovered ways to save more than a third on my auto insurance, and also applied for a substantial tax-averaging return.

God has also helped me find things to furnish our apartment. He made color and obviously loves it—judging from his use of it. He knows better than we do what goes with what, what complements, what sets off, and what will help any of us feel at home. I don't regard God as too busy to get involved in such matters and to guide my thinking, my shopping, and my arranging of a home.

Do some of these matters—a few dollars saved on car insurance, the length of time your kids' tennis shoes last— seem too trivial for prayer? In the shoestring budgets of most divorced women, it is just such things that spell the difference between comfort and desperation.

Having More Than Enough

You may be thinking that this doesn't apply to you. It can, for having more than enough is part of God's plan for his people. When the apostle Paul wrote to the Corinthian Christians who were giving an offering to the poor, he assured them that they would always have enough to be generous (2 Corinthians 9:11).

As you read the Old Testament, you can't help but notice this principle of more than enough, for it was written into the way of life of the people of Israel. God told them that they had more than enough time and that they were to spend one day each week in the leisure of worship. He told them that they had more than enough money and property and that they were to give away large sums, much more than the tithe we speak of today. Of course, part of what they gave went to support the social welfare of the day and is comparable to part of the taxes we pay.

God's principles about the extra, the more than enough, have not changed. Some people regard tithing and Sunday observance as optional, if and when they ever get enough money stored away or enough time to be quiet. But that isn't how it works. You decide that you *will* live according to God's laws and then you see how he works.

Tithing

One enormous choice you will make in your home is what you will do about giving to the Lord. As the children and I moved into our apartment in the fall of 1978, I had no idea how we were going to survive financially.

In that fragile time, I felt great dependence on the Lord. I had always tithed my money and wasn't about to stop then. I was running my bank account right down to empty every payday, and the tithe could have bought some necessary items. Yet, every two weeks, I felt a thankfulness that we were still alive, were still paying our bills, that we had enough—and yes, more than enough. I was reminded of the widow's oil that didn't run out. And I was thankful I could demonstrate to my children that the God who I said was real was concerned about us, that I could show them that Christian faith works in the bad times as well as in the good.

I was also thankful for the luxury of regularly demonstrating, "We have more than enough. We have money to give away." That is a luxury, you know, for someone as strapped as I was. And I was often reminded of Paul's words, "You will always have enough to be generous."

As my earnings increased, so did my contributions to church and missions groups. And it was unavoidable once in a while to think, "That money could have gone a long way toward a downpayment on a house." Yet I don't really think I would have had the downpayment or that we would have fared as well if I had not tithed. I knew what all tithers know—that the Lord helps them to manage better on the ninety percent than they would on the hundred percent.

Leisure

Home is a place for your total self. Your home belongs to you, and one way you know that something belongs to you is if you are not its servant. No matter how busy you are, you can have some periods of leisure, if you believe you can, if you believe that time was made for people and not people for time, if you believe that work is for people, not people for work. As Jesus said, "The Sabbath was made for man, not man for the Sabbath" (Mark 2:27).

The Bible says that God rested after his six days of creative activity. The period of rest was basic to the work and life of the people of Israel—the weekly day of worship and rest, the special Sabbaths, the seventh part of the crop, the seventh year for a field, and after seven times seven years, a Year of Jubilee in which rest was given to people and property that were in bondage.

Unfortunately, real leisure is not very much a part of contemporary Sunday observance. Leisure is not merely the absence of work. Rather, leisure is an attitude in which you look at the world in a special way. It is possible to work so hard in your "leisure" activities that you are never quiet. True leisure is a pursuit of reality that leads you beyond the demands of every day and adds a new dimension to your life.

In his book *Leisure: The Basis of Culture*, Josef Pieper suggests that leisure is expressed in three ways:

1. It is a form of silence.
2. It appears as an attitude of contemplative celebration.
3. It runs at right angles to work.

Leisure is a form of silence, of that silence which is the prerequisite of the apprehension of reality; only the silent hear and those who do not remain silent do not hear. Silence . . . is the soul's power to "answer" to the reality of the world. . . . For leisure is a receptive attitude of mind, a contemplative attitude.[4]

This attitude of leisure may seem incongruous with your schedule, and you may think that I just don't understand about your life. Don't count on it. I lived through extreme pressures on many levels, and I know that it is absolutely necessary to have some times, however brief, in which you have nothing that you must do.

When I was a child, my father used to tell me, "If you are so busy that you don't have some time to do nothing, you are too busy." I think he was right. And probably because of his feeling about this, I was particularly impressed a few years later in high school, when I read W.H. Davies' poem:

What is this life if, full of care,
We have no time to stand and stare?

Standing and staring isn't highly regarded today, but I would recommend it. Superactivism is in, and I would discourage it. Some people are so overscheduled that they are candidates for a breakdown. And if it happens, they won't be any good to anyone.

During the 1960s, we lived four years in Quito, Ecuador. The altitude there is 9,200 feet, before you climb any hills. At that time, doctors didn't know nearly as much about altitude limitations as they do now. One thing I knew for sure was that I just didn't have enough oxygen in Quito to do half of what I wanted to. And I had no intention of ruining my health. So I rather carefully guarded the energy I had and tried to apportion it to what mattered most. And I learned a great deal in that experience about insisting on what is important, even if that means going against the norm. For the norm in our community in Quito was high activity.

Only you can decide what is leisure for you. Only you can decide whether you are pushing dangerously hard and whether you need to make some basic changes in the way you live.

Leisure in its true meaning is not an option, but a necessity. For in times of true leisure, we celebrate life in the knowledge that we are children of God, that we are free people who do not have to work all the time. This freedom is very much like the freedom of tithing. The observance of both will do something for your life that can be accomplished in no other way.

Of course, a major aspect of an observance of leisure is worship. In your home, I hope you will see Sunday as a special day. Your example of going to church regularly, of your taking part in some way, is something your children will not forget.

On the other hand, if they see you as a woman who is totally tied to a schedule, someone who cannot celebrate life, someone who does not worship, someone who never has enough of time and money, they will know that you are not free, that you are not the loved child of a caring heavenly Father. And if mother is not a free person, they must not be free either. They too must be slaves.

I know that the nature of work has changed dramatically in recent years. People rested on the seventh day from six days of hard labor. Now so many people do sedentary work that they need to be active to feel relaxed and leisurely. However, your plans for Sunday rest should not preclude going to church—and to the same church, most of the time. Wandering around just won't do it, especially for your children.

Home and Your Children

Home is where you will reorganize the expressions of your individuality. And you will do it with a ready audience—your children—watching and wondering what Mother is up to now. They will see change happening; they will notice that Mother is doing some things differently than when Dad was around.

Recently I asked my daughter, Cathy, how she felt in the first couple of years after the divorce. She said that in the first year, especially, our apartment didn't feel like home—partly, I'm sure, because she was resisting the idea of it *being* home. Both she and Will found it very difficult to live in an apartment after being in a house for so long. In their thinking, apartment living meant inferior or poor or disadvantaged.

In the first months, Cathy was away at college most of the time, and Will was a sophomore in high school. I knew he wasn't happy about living where we did and, even more, that he was suffering from the separation in the family. What I didn't understand was his resistance to my efforts to make an attractive home for us. After several months, he realized his need to talk with a man about his feelings, and he went to the psychologist who had been such a help to me.

When Will's resistance to my decorating the apartment surfaced, the psychologist asked, "Did you want your mother to hang up black curtains?" Will nodded yes.

Will told me later that he was concerned because we were not appearing to feel as bad as we did feel, or ought to feel, about the divorce. To him, showing that we felt bad meant that we should make little effort to normalize life. To me, the badness needed to be submerged so that the goodness of life could begin to resurface.

Don't be surprised if your children are in conflict with you about seemingly insignificant things in your home. They may feel pulled in several directions at once by love, loyalty, anger, grief, embarrassment, and confusion. But at base may be something that has great significance.

Early in 1984, I heard a psychologist on TV talking about teenage suicide. He said it is highest in societies where there is low family bonding, low religious commitment, high achievement orientation, and high suppression of anger. He felt that North American society, on the average, met these qualifications.

Transfer his comments to the home plagued by divorce, and you can see that our children are threatened by depression, if not suicide. I think his four categories are excellent ones for the single parent to follow—in reverse. We should work toward:

1. high family bonding
2. high religious commitment
3. low achievement orientation
4. low suppression of anger

All of these need some qualification as we think of them in a Christian context.

High family bonding does not mean that the family does everything together. It is not advocating a symbiotic dependency. Rather, bonding means that people are emotionally in touch with one another, that they know each other's needs, fears, and feelings of happiness. They have enough shared experiences to create a bond of places and people as well as a bond of intimate sharing.

High religious orientation means training your children in the Word of God. It means church attendance and participation. It means genuine personal faith in God through his Son, Jesus Christ. It means showing your children that faith has bearing on your life and theirs, that God is a present reality.

Low achievement orientation does not mean that anything goes. Rather, it means that what the child *achieves* is not as important as who he or she *is*. It means that you will not reject your child—ever—because he or she fails to compete favorably with another child. It means that your child's acceptability, now and in the future, does not depend on superior performance.

Low suppression of anger does not mean that the child is constantly venting anger. It does mean that when your child is angry, he or she is allowed to express that anger in an appropriate way, that you do not say, "You shouldn't be mad about that." If your child is angry, the feeling isn't going to go away because you say it should.

This type of atmosphere is one *you* create within your home. That you don't have a husband anymore and that the children don't have a father present does not need to negate the strength of these factors in your home. Yes, you may feel the family bonding is shot to pieces, but your children are not responsible for that. You may think you aren't responsible for it, either. Yet even if you aren't, you do have the obligation to normalize as soon as you can, to strengthen the bonds in the family that lives within your home.

Children often tend to feel that they don't have family anymore because one parent is gone. Those children need even more your demonstration of love and loyalty that says to them, "I am for you—no matter what!" Every child needs to live around someone who is just crazy about him or her. That is true for the best of situations; it is doubly true for yours.

Emotional Climate

Your home can be a place for dying or living, for wilting or blooming, for anxiety or peace, for discouragement or affirmation, for criticism or approval, for profane disregard or reverence, for suspicion or trust, for blame or forgiveness, for alienation or closeness, for violation or respect, for carelessness or caring.

By your daily choices, you will make your home what you want it to be. You cannot avoid these choices. If you choose not to think about them, you are deciding for the negative results that will surely happen. If you daily determine to move in positive directions, you will progress, if ever so slowly.

The family suffering divorce is in a position comparable to the poor man in Jesus' parable—the one who was attacked, robbed, beaten, and left to die. The man may have seen or heard the priest and the Levite passing by— but he could do nothing about their indifference. Then the Samaritan came along and *really saw* the man's condition, and the Samaritan cared. He stopped and got down beside the wounded man.

A home that has endured divorce is wounded, confused, grieving, often robbed of material assets, and usually alone. No one wants to look, much less get too close. People want to tell you, "Be normal. Be a miracle. Be well tomorrow." But it just doesn't happen.

Because other people don't want to look at your hurts, you may decide that you won't look either. You decide that life will be normal if you just put on an act of normalcy. Or maybe people have held out false solutions to you—solutions that you knew wouldn't work; but wanting to be accepted, you tried to go along.

Your home needs someone to really see, to administer oil to the wounds, to provide a place of recovery, some financial help, some warm caring. Yes, you need someone. But there may be no one. My children and I felt very much alone, particularly because some people we thought should have cared or helped didn't want to get near us. And so I became the primary Samaritan for my children, as you will probably be for yours.

For my children and me, home was the dark soil where the seeds fell and grew. It was the cocoon where the caterpillars began to change into butterflies. Home was the safe and protected place where we could be ourselves, could share the pain as well as the joy, could be free to grow, to recover, to help one another.

Home became a refuge in a way it never had been. Yes, home was far different from before—and different didn't mean all bad. In fact, we all knew that some things were much better, that we were becoming stronger people.

Home is where you as the mother need to establish a Christian atmosphere. In some "Christian" homes, by the time a divorce occurs, vile incidents have taken place that leave no doubt about a personal devil. If that has been true in your home, and if your children are aware of the awful things that have transpired, these acts have become part of the norm for them. Don't let that continue. Outrageous and evil actions are not part of a Christian home, but your children will know that only if you teach them. Profanity and an arrogance toward God are not compatible with a Christian home. Nor are cheating, infidelity, lying, or irresponsibility about money.

Gracious Spirit, dwell with me;
I myself would gracious be;
And with words that help and heal
Would They life in mine reveal;
And with actions bold and meek
Would for Christ my Savior speak.

Gracious Spirit, Dwell with Me

Without taking an artificially holy stance, you do need to settle firmly that certain things will or will not be part of your home, because you are seeking to honor God in your way of living together. Then you need to follow through just as firmly, watching that your own behavior and attitudes are consistent with what you have stated as a purpose.

Setting Borders

If your home is to be a place for both you and your children, you need to set the borders for what you want to accomplish. You need emotional borders, borders of tradition and custom. For home to feel like home, you all need to decide what you want to do and be together.

If you wander around with nothing in mind, that is what will happen. As the adult, *you* are responsible, even if you don't always feel like it. You are the one to visualize what home will mean for your family.

As I worked on this chapter, I came in my Bible reading to a story in Joshua that took on a new meaning for me. Joshua had led the children of Israel into the Promised Land. Each tribe was given an inheritance, a future home, but that land would be theirs only as they won it. Five of the tribes had already moved into their new homes, but seven had not. As the congregation assembled, Joshua said to them:

> *How long will you wait before you begin to take possession of the land that the LORD, the God of your fathers, has given you? Appoint three men from each tribe. I will send them out to make a survey of the land and to write a description of it, according to the inheritance of each. Then they will return to me. . . . After you have written descriptions of the seven parts of the land, bring them here to me and I will cast lots for you in the presence of the LORD our God.*
> —Joshua 18:3-4, 6

And what the people wrote down was filled with detail—cities, villages, hills, waters, directions. It was a case of, "What you see is what you get." In walking around their land, they put its borders into their consciousness. Their land now possessed definite form, dimension, size, physical characteristics, and it seemed more obtainable than before.

You can do the same thing in relation to your home. It is important to decide what you want. To do this you need to establish the borders of safety, of traditions, of emotional expression, of a sense of the future. There is a larger life ahead than you can see just now.

Let home be a star to follow. Not all the stars fell; some still shine for you and your children. You need to place them in your sky for those days when everything goes wrong, when the walls start to close in on you and home seems an inhospitable place.

It is on those days that the plans you make for your home, those ideals, will matter tremendously, as you again promise yourself and God that you are going ahead even if you did skin your knee and stub your toe again—even if you fell flat.

Home and Sacrifice

Any good mother often puts the needs of her children ahead of her own. As an adult, you can delay gratification of many of your own needs. Children don't have much capacity for this. In fact, sometimes they just can't do it. They need attention *now* to their emotional needs. Their sense of urgency is too great to be put off—for an answer, for comfort, for advice, for encouragement, for guidance that only a loving adult can give.

For you as a divorced mother, home is the primary place where you will sacrifice for others. Sacrifice is an old-fashioned word that has gone out of style. It is not easy to put aside your own preferences and needs and give to other people. And yet that is what Christians are called to do.

For you as a divorced mother, that call comes in more demanding ways than when there are two functioning parents. You not only have to deal with the needs and demands of today, but you also have to try to put together the brokenness of yesterday and last year and five years ago and move toward a newly defined future. If you have little money to work with, you are operating under considerable pressure. This means you are called upon not only to sacrifice but also to do it with grace.

Some people think it is unhealthy for a single parent to sacrifice her needs in favor of the child. Taking this as a premise, these people have suggested all sorts of behaviors as acceptable, including some that the Christian should consider immoral. The tone of the world today is that gratification should not be delayed, that an adult needs satisfaction now. That the adult is more important than the child. That the adult needs the appearance of normality *now*. The quick fix. No matter what. The good feeling.

I guess I sacrificed a great deal for my children, but I didn't think much about it. I rather regarded it as deferment. God has been doing his work in me during these many years since the divorce. I have been growing as I have tried to provide what my children have needed. Now that the years of extreme pressure are past, I have more time and energy to devote to my own interests. I think I still have some life in me, and I also have the satisfaction that I did what was needed for the people I loved most.

If your self-sacrifice is done in the spirit of Jesus, you will not feel like a victim. Jesus also made demands, as you will remember. He let people minister to him at times. If you are giving of yourself for your children, they should be able to see more than the act. They should come to understand your motivation and your long look toward the future. And they should also sacrifice for you now and then, depending on their age and resources. For you all are growing and healing, and growth requires balance. It demands more than good soil. It needs the light of day and the dark of night. It needs the dryness of sunny days and the nourishment from rainy days.

The balance in self-sacrifice is embodied in Jesus' act of washing the disciples' feet. He did something that they needed in an immediate physical sense. But even more, he provided an example of how they were to live in relationship to one another. Self-sacrifice of this kind does not make you a martyr but an example. And the example of a godly, caring, and loving mother is indeed powerful.

❦ Taking Charge at Home

Determine your priorities for your home.

What I Want to Happen at Home	How I Will Begin
1.	1.
2.	2.
3.	3.
4.	4.
5.	5.
6.	6.

CHAPTER FIVE

YOUR CHILDREN'S NEEDS

The best thing you can do for your
fellow, next to rousing his
conscience, is—not to give him
things to think about, but to wake
things up that are in him; or say, to
make him think things for himself.

—George MacDonald

A bout one year after the divorce, I surprised myself by purchasing an art print of a white tiger. It shows the head and shoulders, a front view in which the cool aquamarine eyes and gently set mouth are the main features.

I looked at that tiger for months before I decided why I had bought it. Yes, it is beautiful, but I am definitely not a cat lover. I finally decided that, in respect to my children, I had become like that tiger: alert, somewhat cool, poised, and ready to defend in an instant. My daughter and son were nineteen and fifteen at the time of the divorce—still terribly vulnerable. They would so soon be into their adult lives, and they had miles of old hurts to travel before they would be ready.

Cathy was eighteen when, before the divorce, we reached the point where our home could no longer function. My reaction to that crisis was obvious, both physically and emotionally. Cathy rather critically said, "My mother, who had all the answers, who helped me through all our moves with her prayers, fell off her pedestal."

I hadn't known I was on one or that it was so highly placed—quite near to God, in Cathy's estimation. And she went through a long time of not really trusting me or my judgment. She knew that she and her brother should live with me, but she definitely felt hostile. I had broken some dreams, some beliefs, some ideas about life. At that time, she wondered if I had broken the home.

Cathy knew the situation at home wasn't ideal, but I had so well concealed the problems that she had no idea how bad they were. She was old enough and smart enough to know that there must be more to the story than I was at first telling her, and before long she was questioning me in a way that couldn't be evaded. She said, "Tell me everything."

Her brother, on the other hand, said, "Don't tell me. I don't want to know."

Each position had to be respected. Yet Will had to learn more in the next year than he wanted to know. Cathy had to work through her own reactions to the present and the past, and she had to do this partly alone, since she was away at school much of the time.

Before and after the divorce, both children watched me as I struggled and, yes, fought my way through the most awful time of my life. When they seemed to wonder at the extremity of the pain, at my most uncool reactions, I told them, "If I could have gone through the breaking of a home with unconcern or only minor hurt, you would really have a problem on your hands!"

What they were watching was the wrenching, agonizing pain of a wife who had married once-for-always and who was now seeing life deliberately torn apart.

Much of what my children saw in me that first year was unattractive; I dealt honestly and openly with my pain, resentment, and fear. Yet as I look back on it, I am glad they were alongside me, for there was in my struggling an authentic quality on which they could draw and build.

Angers and fears and hurts had to be expressed. Dreams and hopes needed rebuilding. Both Cathy and Will felt a sense of shame that their parents were divorced. This was something that happened to other people from far different backgrounds, not to people who had been so involved in the church. No one in our families was divorced, and the children had never considered it a possibility.

They felt as if the faults of their family had suddenly gone public. Cathy especially sensed a lack of privacy. Neither of them wanted to be an object of pity.

Also, they both felt a definite imbalance. A home should have two parents, not one. This was more difficult for Will, because it mean that he and I were the only ones home, since Cathy was away at school eight months each year. He needed the role model of a man in the home.

One night when he was sixteen, feeling very much alone, he looked at me with dreadful pain in his eyes and said, "Who have I got? I've got you and I've got Cathy." And then he sat at the kitchen table and cried. I cried too. And long after he had gone to sleep, I was awake, praying, arguing with God, begging him to be a Father to Will, to meet his needs and to send someone who could help him.

That night God reminded me of some of the best men in the Bible—men we think may not have had their fathers to finish raising them. Heading this list is Joseph, who seemed to have everything against him—being sold by his own family members to a foreign people, living as a teenager in a godless society, suffering further injustices, and yet knowing the inner presence of God in a way that stabilized him and readied him for his unusual position as governor of Egypt (Genesis 37–47).

Samuel was taken from his home at a young age to live with the priest Eli, who had not been a good father to his own sons. And from a tender age Samuel knew the presence of God in his life (1 Samuel 1–24).

It is likely that John the Baptist did not have his parents during part of his maturing years, since they were so old when he was born. Yet of him Jesus said that there was none better born of woman (Luke 7:26-28).

Daniel was another—perhaps in captivity with his family and yet certainly without their support as he was brought into the palace to be trained to serve the Persian Empire. He too experienced the presence of the living God in a remarkable way (Daniel 1–12).

After thinking about these men, I talked with Will about what I felt the Lord had given me as an answer. I was hesitant in what I said because I didn't want him to think that I believed God in heaven was the same as a father who could be alongside him every day. Although Will didn't say much at the time, he seemed to understand what I was trying to tell him, and in subsequent months and years, I could see that he had opened himself to God's work within him.

I tried not to use my children as a dumping ground or lean on them emotionally. I tried not to make them adults in the home. But at those times I lacked answers or stability, they felt that lack. There were times when no one had the answers and no one felt stable—times when we were all slowly trudging or fighting our way forward.

Other times, either Cathy or Will had the answer we needed. I had long known that parents can learn from their children. But during those early years, I experienced this in a special way. Because Cathy and Will are Christians, the Spirit of God ministers through them as surely as he does through other believers. And I felt the oneness of the body of Christ in our home.

These years have drawn us close together in understandings that will reach into the future. We know God is, and that he is the rewarder of those who come to him in faith. We know each other deeply and have forged a very special love.

What Do They Need?

"See that you do not look down on one of these little ones. For I tell you that their angels in heaven always see the face of my Father in heaven."
—Matthew 18:10

What do children of divorce need? They need at least one adult who functions as a parent. Turn that around. They need at least one parent in the home who is an adult in relation to the children. They need someone who is really committed to them, to their welfare and future, and to the healing that needs to take place in their lives.

Normalcy
Children of divorce need an atmosphere of normalcy and stability. They need space and time to grow. They don't need more pressure and stress. During the first eighteen months after the children and I moved, I worked too much just to keep us alive. I had been full-time on my job a short

time and wasn't making a spectacular wage. So at night and on weekends I did freelance projects at home. Most of my weekdays went from six in the morning to midnight. Still, if my children needed to talk, I stopped working. They came first.

As my earnings increased, I was able to move toward a more normal work schedule, doing less freelance work. This was good for Cathy and Will, since they had gotten very restless seeing me work so much. They wanted me to sit more and have more time to talk or just say nothing together, as we used to do. They wanted life to feel normal again.

I got the idea. When I began to have more time, I bought some handwork projects, embroidery for which I had to sit and be quiet and look just like they thought Mother should look. Three of the pieces I worked on during that time are hanging on our walls. To me they have a double design— the patterns themselves and the configuration of quietness my children needed.

Health

Your children need an emotionally healthy home. They need you to attend to your own attitudes and to set your life in the direction of normal. The longer you were married, the more difficult this may be to do.

During the first year, I often felt that I had been severely victimized. Fortunately, I was so busy I didn't have much time to think about it. But I knew then, and know more now, that a mother who feels victimized had better work through and out of that feeling. If she does not and if her children move into adulthood feeling like victims, they will marry victims, and the downward process will go right on.

I was determined to break, in myself and in my children, some behavior patterns that had been in motion on both sides of the family. And I could not ask my children to do what I would not do myself.

This meant some restructuring of how Cathy, Will, and I related to each other. It meant some restructuring of how we related to our relatives. It meant a conscious change in certain attitudes and feelings about ourselves, our home, and our friends.

Why was all of this necessary? Because I was determined that my children would begin their adult lives as confident, prepared, happy, and mature people. They would not be victims—unsure, fearful, self-conscious, skeptical—but people who have seen God alive on this side of Easter, who know he cares and acts for people today.

To accomplish all of that, I needed to take a good look at my relatives to see how they functioned in relation to one another. So do you. Don't limit yourself to your own side of the family. Look at your ex-husband's family too, since they are still relatives of your children. Watch how they get along, how they pressure one another. You may observe some interesting and less-than-healthy tendencies that have had an impact on you and your children.

For instance, you may find certain values out of balance. One common imbalance in our society is for appearance to take a place of importance above people, above reality.

You may see tendencies toward self-deprecation. You may find family members who lack self-confidence and share those uncertainties with others, leading those others likewise to doubt their worth. This is particularly damaging when older people influence the young to feel inferior.

You might see a blame mentality, a kind of emotional dumping in which blame is generously shared with those who had nothing to do with the problem. Don't let people dump on you or your children.

You may discover a lack of direct communication in your extended family. You may see people trying to convey messages through others, rather than delivering them directly. Mothers make excellent message carriers, just because they usually accept the job. So do children. Don't let this happen. Insist that your children learn how to communicate directly, and that family members not use you or your children to send their messages.

If any of these remind you of traits in your families, take another look. You'll probably find other tendencies that you have taken for granted because they are the way all your relatives—or his—behave. Each family has patterns of behavior they find acceptable. But that doesn't make those patterns healthy. What you need now is to move toward optimum emotional health for yourself and your children.

Protection

In being as protective as I was, I was behaving in a way that is at crosscurrents with today's general thought about children.

> American society is becoming not so much antichild as a-child. Growing numbers of working couples and single parents are pushing their offspring into the periphery of their lives, dependent on the kindness of strangers to keep their youngsters safe and help them develop for great chunks of their childhood. . . . Something has gone drastically wrong when it is so difficult for parents to provide adequate care for small children.[1]

In her excellent book *Children Without Childhood*, Marie Winn discusses an alteration in the concept of childhood joys and boundaries.

Something has happened to blur the formerly distinct boundaries between childhood and adulthood, to weaken the protective membrane that once served to shelter children from precocious experience and sorrowful knowledge of the adult world. All over the country newly single mothers are sitting down with their children and making what has come to be known as The Speech: "Look, things are going to have to be different. We're all in this together and we're going to have to be partners."

Marie Winn sees the attitude toward childhood as reflecting the social change of the past generation. The lives of children mirror the lives of adults. It is a circular pattern, with adults and children each responding to the changes observed in the other.

For instance, as today's children impress adults with their sophisticated ways, adults begin to change their ideas about children and their needs; that is they form new conceptions of childhood. Why, these tough little customers don't require protection and careful nurture! No longer need adults withhold information about the harsh realities of life from children. No longer need they hide the truth about their own weaknesses. Rather, they begin to feel it is their duty to prepare children for the experiences of modern life. However, as adults act less protectively . . . and as they expose children to the formerly secret underside of their lives . . . those former innocents grow tougher, perforce, less playful and trusting, more skeptical—in short, more like adults.[2]

When I worked on Brian Stiller's book *A Generation Under Siege*, I was deeply moved by the following true story:

85

It was late as Hank quietly slipped upstairs. Mom would be sleeping and he didn't want to disturb her. But she was awake.

"Hank, please come here for a moment," she called. He went into her bedroom and immediately sensed something was wrong.

Hank's dad had left a few years ago. Recently, his mom had been dating another man.

"Hank," his mom said, "we plan to get married." Hank was pleased. This would be a good deal for Mom. But he wasn't ready for the bombshell.

"Hank, there is something else you need to know." He looked up, confused by the threat of danger.

"There is one condition. He only wants me. You see, Hank, soon you will be finishing high school and then you'll go on to college, and then what will there be for me? O Hank, you do understand, don't you?"

Hank understood, all right. That Christmas he walked away from the only parent he had thought loved him.[3]

Your children need your protective love and loyalty—all the way through their teenage years and beyond.

Control

Your children need you to be in control of the family and to be *for* them, no matter what. They need your care and involvement in all areas of their lives. They need rules and discipline and the idealism that helps them move ahead into their own adult lives. They need to understand that thoughtless self-indulgence now may mar their lives in the years to come.

They need to see an example of self-discipline and devotion to love, truth, and duty. That example is you, Mom.

They do not need to live in a home dominated by television. Except for isolated specials and sporting events, it would be hard to make much of a case for the benefits of commercial television. Even the news can be destructive. Who can internalize that much conflict and grief? People today see more human suffering in one week than most people of a century ago saw in a lifetime. And yet, since there is usually nothing we can do about the suffering we see on the screen, we become more and more sterile in relation to it. We cauterize our hearts, we anesthetize our feelings, and this has an effect in our personal relationships.

In 1970, our family returned from four years in Ecuador. Stunned by the changes that had taken place in society, especially as they were reflected in what we were seeing on television, I wrote the following:

the tube

They enter with unsmiling eyes
these determined strangers.

And we
trapped by the necessary
bored by the optional
confused by the choices
are stunned by these strangers.

Strangers we will never know nor help
though we try, for we formulate
our partially valid solutions
to their partially explained situations
of war and peace, of life and love.

They shout, they preen, they slouch,
they mumble expertise,
these stranger supermen.

They need for us to need them.
They are paid to make us think we need them
and paid yet more
when we don't stop to think there is a choice.

As we live with the impossibility
of building fleeting images
into stability,
the strangers come
and go
and we are left
with neither memory of a touch
nor promise of a friend.

Reality

Children are natural tragedians—especially teenagers. When it comes to feeling tragedy, most of them could match Shakespeare wound for wound. His great advantage was his profound sense of history. Your sense of past and future is precisely what your children need from you, since they don't have the backdrop of years and experience against which to position their fears. Because of this, their small tragedies quickly can move out of the context of reality into fantasy. The slightest problem can be magnified a thousand times to an imaginary outcome for which they will then grieve.

In addition to this normal tendency, your children bear the added burden of having experienced the real tragedy—the brokenness of their family and the ensuing pain. They need your help with this real grief, into which they may inject elements of unreality, just because of their age. They may feel a fear of a graduation or a wedding or other family gathering that all their relatives will attend. They may fear that divorce will keep them from marrying into the right kind of family. They may fear that there will not be enough money to educate them properly. They may fear rejection from people they like or love—a real fear based on the way they've already been treated by some. But to enlarge the fear will only add hesitation to the child's behavior and heighten the likelihood of rejection or avoidance.

You who are also wounded are the one to deal with each child's sense of tragedy. Never underestimate or deal casally with the feelings. Try to illuminate their fears with the perspective of reality; try to help your children see each situation in as clear and favorable a light as is honest. But then always be sure you have dealt with the feelings, however irrational they may seem. The feelings will last long after the facts are forgotten, and unresolved negative feelings will turn inward and become enemies to your children for years to come.

Love
What do your children need most? Your love in action. In *How to Really Love Your Teenager*, Dr. Ross Campbell comments about the failure of parents to show love to their teenagers:

> Very few teenagers are fortunate enough to feel truly loved and accepted as they should be. It is true that most parents have deep feelings of love toward their teenagers. They assume, however, that they naturally and effectively convey this love. This is indeed the greatest error parents make today. For most parents are simply not transmitting or conveying their own heartfelt love to their teenagers. The reason is that they do not know how.[4]

As a psychiatrist specializing in child care, Dr. Campbell works with children whose parents have met every need except the need of felt love. As Christians, we are given a standard by which we can know if we are loving others: "This is how we know what love is: Jesus Christ laid down his life for us. And we ought to lay down our lives for our brothers. If anyone has material possessions and sees his brother in need but has no pity on him, how can the love of God be in him?" (1 John 3:16-17).

We are to lay down our lives for our children. If a woman has enough to sustain her life emotionally and physically and sees her children in need and closes her heart against them, refusing to meet their needs, how can it be said that the love of God dwells in her?

When you come to know yourself intimately and decide what matters most to you, you will discover times when you are called to give up or delay what you most want for love of others, for love of God. Throughout the Scriptures, God generally only asked for one thing from people—what they wanted most. He asks the same of you. But you don't lose by doing things God's way. He is in the business of perfecting us, of making a people for his name. That is far more important than getting what you think you want right now.

The Frontier of Need

After my divorce I was reminded of God's care for single parents in the Bible. I was particularly impressed with the story of Hagar and the son she had by Abraham, at Sarah's suggestion (Genesis 16–21).

Hagar had been badly used, in a scheme devised by a woman and consented to by a man. God would not change his plan to accommodate Sarah's scheme. But neither did he forget his lovingkindness to the afflicted, Hagar and Ishmael, who were thrown out of the home by Sarah after the primary heir, Isaac, was born. God came to Hagar with tenderness, with provision, and with a promise of life and future for her and for her teenage son.

When God heard Ishmael crying, he told Hagar to get up and hold Ishmael in her arms. God doesn't wipe tears when we can. He would need Hagar's love in order to fulfill his promise for Ishmael. Your children need your love in the same way.

Being misused by another person, as Hagar was, does not mean that you are cut off from the promise of God. It may mean that those promises will be stated and restated to you in ways that you never would have heard in ordinary circumstances. And you may take hold of a sense of the future for yourself and your children in a way that would not have happened in more favorable surroundings.

It is when we come to what Oswald Chambers calls "the frontier of need," where we know our limitations, that God's redemptive purposes have a chance best to take effect in our lives. Those purposes were there all along, but we may not have seen them because we were not at the frontier of need. After all, no one goes there voluntarily, willingly. We think of it as a bad place, a place of vulnerability and exposure and want, and we avoid it.

Hagar couldn't avoid being there. I couldn't either. And now you can't. You will discover that God is always at the frontier of need, outside the camp of regular living, where hurting people are.

We read in Hebrews 13 that Jesus was offered up on the cross outside the camp, in the place where animal sacrifices were offered, in the place where lepers and other unclean were kept. It is in this place today, outside the niceties and safe circumstances, out at the frontiers of need, that Jesus meets us—not just divorced people, but all people who are finally brought there by the circumstances of their lives and by their own inadequacies. People arrive there in a variety of ways, none of them pleasant. But the possibilities on the other side are great, for both you and your children.

A pastor who has worked with many divorced people and their children once said, "God must especially love divorced people because of the way he cares for them." I have known that care now for many years. But there is no forgetting that I have also known what it is like outside the camp.

Who else has been outside the camp? Hagar out in the desert and the widow who gave to Elijah were both at the end of their resources, at the frontier of need. But then so was Abraham at the frontier, and he wasn't a single parent—though he may have felt like one as he climbed the mountain with Isaac, preparing to sacrifice the boy. God let him continue his preparations right to the raising of his arm to slay Isaac. We know that God wanted his willingness. But Abraham didn't know that—he had to go right to the edge.

For it is at the edge that God can work in our lives. You got there through divorce. Other people arrive at this point by various experiences. It is important for you not to think God has special rules and ways of working just for you. God works according to his own character and purposes. Right now you are in a place where he can make those evident in your life.

It matters very much that you learn to discern the leading of the Lord and then communicate this to your children. They need to know that you are walking with God, that you care about his word and commandments, and that you have a sense of future and hope within his purposes for your life. They need to know that you pray, that you depend on the Lord and are exercising faith in a time when it is not easy. They need to be drawn into your spiritual experiences so they can observe how a Christian behaves under pressure. This behavior, commonly called courage, is a command given to those at the frontier of risk or suffering.

What you as a newly divorced mother do about most everything is an illustration to your children. You are being healed. You are solving new problems. You are making a new way of life. You are both building and rebuilding. You are drawing on your meager resources of courage to do the ordinary. Everything you do is obvious to your children because so much of it is different from before.

A Long Way Up

I needed help when my children were nineteen and fifteen, when they were twenty and sixteen. I felt the pressure of the short time before they would be on their own. I remember days when I was more than a little angry because no one seemed to care. Of course, what I really needed was the normalcy of life without divorce and with a father in the home. Lacking these, I felt the need of some caring adults to reach out to my children and give them what they needed. I am more aware now than I was then that this type of assistance is difficult to offer. And the problem was compounded in our case by the fact that I have few relatives.

Now, many years later, I have to say that we somehow survived—*had* to survive—with whatever level of help we found. And I do see the impact that a few kind and loving people had on Cathy and Will, even when the time spent together was short. Their needs often seemed to get short-changed.

Today Cathy and Will are confident, strong, and balanced. I believe the resources that seemed so insufficient at the time were multiplied by the One who took a few loaves and fishes and fed thousands, by the One who kept the oil in the widow's pitcher from running dry until she had enough.

One person consistently went far beyond any reasonable expectation of self-giving. David Parker, who is now my son-in-law, was still in college and just moving into his own adult life at the time. Yet with great maturity he cared for, supported, challenged, and gave hope to Cathy and Will in ways that I could not. He saw what they could become, and that gave them the courage to plod on when they didn't feel like it, when they could have given up hope of life ever again being good.

I'm glad David was along with us during these years, for he is a mountain climber, as is Will, and what we all went through can be compared to climbing a mountain. We have each had our own mountains, and yet we have been near enough to quickly reach a helping hand to one another. Mountain climbing is known for more than the exhilarating thrill of arrival on top. The climbers also experience pain, suspense, careful maneuvering, exhaustion, and realization that it is a long way down, as well as a long way up.

The Contradictions of Love

What do your children need? That depends, of course, on what they are lacking. But you can be sure they need some very contradictory things. They need a sense of normalcy, and yet they need to know that divorce is not normal.

They need some cushioning where they are in pain, but they do not need a crutch that will prevent them from becoming strong.

They need to understand, to some extent, what was wrong in the home, and yet they also need to appreciate that there were many good things in the years past, that they have a background on which they can draw.

They need to know that the anger they feel is perfectly normal. You may even have to lead them to resolution of their anger against you. And this takes some doing, because one part of you is a sensitive human being who doesn't like the attitudes expressed against you by a hostile child. The other side of you is a caring parent who knows that the anger is not so much against you as against the broken home and the altered way of life with which this child must now cope, though he or she did nothing to cause it.

Just as you may feel reluctant to reenter the social scene, so your teenage children may not want to attend parties and church functions for a while. The more prominent your family has been in church, the more embarrassed your children will be.

At this point, your children need more than your encouragement. They need your example. Peers are no help. Other adults are reticent to reach out. Most relatives tend to keep their distance. If this is true for you, your children may gain courage to move out only as they see you doing the same. As they see you regularly attending church and beginning to participate in some form of service, they may realize that they can do this too.

When your children see normalcy gradually begin to flow again in your life, they will let it become part of their lives also.

Be a Functioning Parent

Children of divorce need at least one parent functioning for them. They do not need to be dispossessed by losing both parents at the same time. Yet this happens to so many children that it is more often the rule than the exception.

Such children lose one parent because he moves away. They lose the other, usually the mother who has custody, because she is out in pursuit of another mate. About the time our home was breaking up, a mother of three children said her husband of twenty years just didn't want the responsibility of being married anymore. "This means," she said angrily, "that women like you and me have to go out and find somebody else!"

I thought, "Honey, speak for yourself!" While I didn't feel any such compulsion, I did understand her feelings. Beyond the turmoil and stigma of divorce is a profound loneliness, a feeling of abandonment and isolation. But rapid remarriage is not a cure for either of these.

If you find yourself desperate for a man, please think about what this pursuit of a mate is teaching your children about their own value, about you, about marriage, about God and his purposes, about the value of human life, about the recovery that needs to take place in all of you. Some women seem to be teaching their children that a man—almost any man—is what counts in life. The role-modeling effects of such a mother will continue into the adult lives of her children.

Know That God Cares

More than anything else, your children need you to work through and resolve your own problems. They need you to put your life in order, piece by piece, and let them know how some of it happened. They need to be able to respect you—your decisions, attitudes, and behavior.

I had a long agenda during those first years. You have a long agenda too. And your children are affected by most of the items on that agenda.

Give your children to God. Give your own self to God. Pray together with your children in honest terms that are appropriate to their age and understanding. Then daily trust God to do his work in all of you.

Those moments when you are totally helpless to aid your children—when you reach out but cannot touch where it hurts—those are the priceless times when you can risk. Pray with your child, asking God to do his work, not suggesting how, but in faith asking for a specific answer for this your beloved child who has a need.

In the few times in each child's life when I have prayed this way, from my extremity and their pain or need, I have always heard the mocking question afterward: "What if God doesn't do anything? Won't you look silly, putting yourself out on a limb before this child? You, the great believer in God!"

But the "What if?" never comes to anything. For a parent's prayer from extremity is God's opportunity to show his love to this little one of six or sixteen.

Your children have angels, and those angels see the face of God every day. Through these ministering spirits or in a direct way, God works in and for your children. God cares about them as much as you do, and he is able to do for them what you cannot do.

❧ Meeting Your Children's Needs

List your children's needs and the ways you and they can begin to meet those needs.

	How to Begin to Meet the Need
Child's Name _____	
Need _____	
Need _____	
Child's Name _____	
Need _____	
Need _____	
Child's Name _____	
Need _____	
Need _____	

CHAPTER SIX

NEVER WHIMPER AT WORK

Teach us, O Lord, to do little things as
though they were great, because of
the majesty of Christ who does them
in us and who lives our life; and to do
the greatest things as though they
were little and easy, because of His
omnipotence.

—Pascal

Everyone knows that in most
people's estimation, to do anything
coolly is to do it genteelly.

—Herman Melville

If you are like most divorced women, you have to work.
If you were married a long time and are new to the work
scene, you may feel unprepared to survive in this new
world. If you have children who live at home, you probably
see work as an interference in your obligation to your
children as well as something that leaves you constantly
exhausted.

You may have no choice about whether you work. But you do have a choice about what work you do and how much and where. You also have a choice about how you feel about that work. Let's consider those options.

Work and Your Children's Needs

If you have preschool children, it's best not to be away from home more than half a day, if you can manage it. If you have school-age children, try to be home during the hours when they are. The before- and after-school hours are crucially important, even to teenagers. After school is a time to talk, eat, and share all kinds of things that don't sound important—but really are. After school is a time when school-age children need daily supervision. The small latchkey kids tug at our sympathies. The big latchkey kids, teenagers, seem more self-reliant. However, they are also more advanced in potential for harming themselves during unsupervised hours.

With the economic pressure you are likely feeling, you may think it is unrealistic even to consider working less than full-time. You may also think that you have to go where the big salaries are. I lived in a suburb of Chicago, and I knew that if I worked in the city, I could earn more—just about enough more to pay for my commuter ticket and the extra clothes I would need. I don't think the extra money would have covered the two hours each day of travel time. And certainly nothing can compensate for the anxiety a mother feels when she is working too far away from her children.

My son was fifteen and beginning his second year in high school when his father and I were divorced. Physically, Will was a big boy then, about six feet tall. But inside, he was hurting and insecure from the break in the family. I was very glad to work only two miles from home. Most days, when he got out of school, he would either call me or ride his bike over and talk to me for a few minutes. If he and a friend had a sudden brainstorm, they could check with me and let me know where they would be. There is no way I could have kept track of him had I been working thirty miles away. And there is no way I could have put a warm supper on the table at any reasonable hour if I had been arriving home at 6:30 in the evening.

As you think about work, begin with the needs of your children, not only their physical needs but also their emotional and mental needs. If you resolve to find employment compatible with meeting those needs, you'll find yourself looking in different places than you otherwise would. You'll find yourself talking with different people about your employment. And in the confidence that you are trying to do what is best for those children whom God so especially loves, you will feel very free to take your specific employment needs to church and prayer groups, to ask their participation with you.

If, on the other hand, you make decisions that leave *you* uncomfortable, you will feel guilty. And you will imagine that people are judging you. There are not many specific things you *have* to do. Yes, you probably have to work. But you can choose where and when.

Don't overlook the growing possibilities for working at home. More and more companies are finding it profitable to employ people who work most of their hours in their own homes.

Consider sharing a job with someone else, another option that seems to be on the increase.

If you have some help with your children from relatives you fully trust, you might consider working long hours one week and then being home the next.

Consider putting two smaller jobs together to come up with one whole. Or consider adding to your income with seasonal work that is near your home.

If you have very young children and if you have the facility for it, you may be able to take care of one or more other children in your home.

You may be able to find freelance work that will supplement your income. Or you may have a skill or hobby that you can turn into dollars.

Your Total Financial Picture

Your paycheck is only one of the primary resources you'll use in putting together your total financial picture. You also need good benefits. Never underestimate the importance of health insurance, life insurance, paid vacation, paid sick days and holidays, disability insurance, and a pension plan. Beyond these, you may also find such benefits as health clubs, child care, a company cafeteria, or a stock plan.

If you are the custodial parent, you are probably receiving child support. You will want to be sure that your children are covered by any available insurances their father has.

While you want to receive all that should come to you, you also want to be fair about what you say you need for your children, and careful about how you spend the support money. Don't try to gouge your former husband. And remember to keep careful accounts, in case you later need to provide proof of how you used the support money.

A caring father will want to provide some extras now and then, beyond the regular child support—major items of clothing, maybe, or a trip to see the grandparents. If your ex-husband is like this, you are fortunate. All too many custodial parents have to cope with the nonsense of a few dollars being deducted from the support check because the other parent wanted to take the child out to eat. Try to establish that the support is a regular amount, to be changed only if the child stays several days with the father.

What about extravagant gifts given to the child to curry favor? If you can communicate with your former husband, urge him to check with you about the needs and wants of the child before buying a large item.

While this book is primarily for women who have custody of their children, it may be that your former husband has primary custody and that you are paying support. Then you need to cooperate with him for the greater benefit of your children. It is so easy for divorced parents to use money to try to buy love or sympathy from their children. Don't try this—it has a way of boomeranging.

Your Ambition and Your Schedule

He who began a good work in you will carry it on to completion until the day of Christ Jesus.

—Philippians 1:6

If you are going to work outside of your home, realize that you cannot fulfill all your ambitions in the first years—especially if you still have children at home. It would be wise to find a job in a stable company in your area. If you find that you like the field of work, then begin to educate yourself in the wider sphere of that kind of job.

For instance, I am a book editor. When I began working full-time, I knew right away that I would have to learn something about the publishing world that was far removed from my office. For me, that meant paying attention to the publishing magazines that came into the office, watching for articles with special application to what we were doing, looking for books that would help me.

The more I learned about publishing, the surer I was that I needed to move into author acquisition. Many editors don't choose to go this direction, but for me it proved to be a good move. And as a side benefit, I experienced more personal growth in my acquisition activity than in any other part of my work.

What kind of work do you do? What is the larger sphere for that job? If you are a sales clerk, you can learn merchandising, with specific application to your kind of trade. If you are selling clothing, you can expand your knowledge about the fashion industry, about fabrics and colors and design.

Do you work for a nonprofit organization? Then learn some of the distinctive characteristics of working for this type of group, be it church or mission or community service.

If you are a teacher, your lines of job enrichment are mostly outlined for you—but not entirely. When my son was in the sixth grade, his teacher was a young man who had grown up in the parochial schools of Chicago and in the process had learned something about the obligation of the advantaged to the disadvantaged. His sixth graders spent two hours each week at a nearby nursing home, visiting with the people, playing games, giving little programs. In these two hours a week, this teacher taught in a way that was also to enrich my son's life. He was the only teacher in the Wheaton school system that year who was doing such a thing. And he was finally called before a group of teachers and board members to explain how he ever found time for such an activity. His response: "We first do what is right, and then we have time for the necessary."

Your Job Description Is Your Friend

As you work, you may see another job in your company that intrigues you. And you may feel rather sure that you would like to move in that direction, should an opening occur. In 1976, I began working half-time at Scripture Press; before long, I knew that if I were to work full-time, I wanted to work in the book division, and I mentioned this to the personnel director.

As you work, you may see ways that you can enrich your job and gain more responsibility. With the approval of a boss who was willing to let me try myself in acquisitions, I slowly moved more and more into that work. After all, I didn't think it was appropriate for me to ask for the job until we all knew that I could do it. After I had shown over a period of time that I could produce, I asked to have my job refactored to show the added responsibility. A few years later, I took on more complicated assignments, asked to have the job refactored again, and received another promotion.

Your job description is your friend. The reason that I could have the jobs refactored is that I had a fairly exact job description. Pay close attention to yours. By knowing what you are responsible for and how you are evaluated, not only by your boss but by the company at large, you will be able to move both up and sideways, should you desire.

As you probably noticed, I *asked* for every move. All good things do not necessarily come to those who sit and wait. But I didn't ask until I felt it was fair and justified.

Your company doesn't owe you a thing, except to pay you what was agreed upon, to provide a decent work environment for what you do, and to give benefits and protections prescribed by law.

Your company does not owe you advancement. It does not owe you salary increases just because you are nice and agreeable. Your company does not owe you expanded opportunities because you have financial need.

Frankly, a divorced mother can be something of a liability for a while, until she gets her life in order. She can be distracted when her children are sick or unhappy.

Your company should give you the opportunity to show what you can do. And then you owe them fair exchange for the bargain made.

Working Overtime

You owe it to yourself to do the quality of work that will bring commendation. But quality of work doesn't mean all kinds of overtime. One woman told me about the hundreds of extra hours she had put in during the last few years. I responded, "You shouldn't do that. A few hours here and there, yes. But excessive hours, no."

I imagine she thought her overtime would be appreciated and that she would be rewarded by a grateful boss. It doesn't work that way. There is a perversity in human nature that makes people appreciate the person who appreciates herself. I suggested to this woman that she would be better off spending more time in going back to school and finishing her master's degree so that she would have a credential to show for the time.

If your job description requires that you do the work of more than one person, it is not accurate. If your extra work means that you do *more* than your job description describes, you are not being fair to the other employees at your company. I am not talking about extra work once in a while in an emergency. I mean the consistent excessive work that makes people in your department look like slouches for merely putting in a full day's work.

Or maybe you're spending excessive time on the job because you're a workaholic. Either way, you're certainly not spending your leisure time and extra energy on personal enrichment. You are making yourself a drudge, as if your main ambition were to stay forever at your present level. The people who move are those who do their present jobs well and who are always looking for new challenges.

By and large, people appreciate what they pay for. Most employers won't pay for excessive overtime they didn't ask for. My guess is that they don't appreciate it either. They may wonder why the workaholics don't have anything better to do with their time.

Working Smarter

I believe in working smarter, not longer. There is a need for increased quality in most jobs. And ideas for quality come from thinking. Which, by the way, reminds me that I *am* guilty of working overtime, after all, since I have spent a fair amount of my own time thinking about ways to improve my performance at work. But while I was thinking, I could also be preparing dinner, running the vacuum, driving to the store.

When you come up with an idea you think would help you or your group to work smarter, develop it to its conclusion. What is the benefit to the company? If the benefit to your employer is not as great as the benefit to you, forget it. Work means product and profits. Even in nonprofit organizations there should be a product of sorts and a measurable profitability.

I found if I could demonstrate that my idea would be good for my company, I could usually sell it. I rather enjoyed that, especially if it was something I particularly wanted. It is good practice to write down ideas that are at all complicated. Your boss has more to do than remember your brainstorms.

If no one pays attention to your ideas the first time around, consider it par for the course. The second time they may hear you, and the third time you may make a sale.

Even after you do, you should remind yourself that most of your ideas are not going to fly right away, and maybe they will never be accepted. No company can implement the suggestions of every employee. So save your energy for your best ideas.

Realism

One of the greatest needs for working women is to see their work scene realistically; you need to see things as they *are*. If you can also see them as they *should* be and if you can combine the two, more power to you. But always begin with seeing events and people as they are.

Many working people—men as well as women—tend to think that because things *should* be a certain way, they really basically *are* this way. If only there were a different administration, things would be as these people want them to be. Such people just don't live in the real world.

So where do you begin in being realistic? For starters, try to understand the company you work for. Learn how it is organized. Know who makes what kinds of decisions. Know how you and other employees are evaluated. Keep a copy of your job description; look at it occasionally to see if it truly reflects what you are doing—I don't mean every last detail of your job, but the general descriptions of levels of responsibility and independent action.

Learn to appreciate the importance of the product—the goods or services offered by your employer. It is your relationship to the product that makes you more or less valuable. If you find you are in a job that has become optional in relation to the product, look right now to see if you can make a move in your company.

Watch what you say and to whom. Don't be known as the company gossip. Don't be a troublemaker. Don't always be on the fringe of cooperation.

If you disagree strongly with something you are asked to do, have a talk with your boss. Respectfully explain why you don't think the order is a good one. If your problem is ethical or moral and has nothing particularly to do with the company structure, you may need to make a lonely decision to leave. But far more often, you will disagree because you just don't think you have been given a wise order, on the basis of the information you possess. A reasonable manager will think twice before asking a hard-working employee to go against her better judgment.

And as you bring your best thinking to bear on a given situation, you are fulfilling your obligation to your manager. You will be appreciated even more if you can outline an alternative way to get the job done. After all, your manager is given the task of fulfilling the job and is probably not wedded to every last detail of the process.

If you are going to be a realistic worker, you need to know that some people tend to dump problems or work on others. Don't let people dump on you. At least, not more than once. If you put up with it in your office, it will increase until it becomes impossible to cope with. Treasure your job description at times when people try to dump their work on you. I am not talking about voluntarily helping a fellow employee who is in a bind or who has a personal problem. We all give such help, now and then—partly because we all *need* it now and then.

Learn the goals of your company; evaluate the ways that your personal working goals correspond with what is expected of you.

Never underestimate the importance of money on the work scene. Money provides the goods or services; money pays salaries and benefits. Do your part to make your company prosperous.

Cool in the Office

When Geraldine Ferraro had to face the press after the disclosures of her income during the 1984 presidential campaign, the *Chicago Tribune* lauded her performance in a front page headline: FERRARO KEEPS COOL.

Last year, a young woman in our company was given a special award for carrying through a project that was far beyond her job description. In presenting the award to her, the president of the company said that she had not lost her cool during the months of extra work.

Whatever you do, keep your cool—especially if you work with or for men. If you don't know how to do it, learn. Since you can't afford to lose your cool more than two or three times a year, save the uncool for things that really matter.

As I thought about keeping cool, I wondered if this is strictly a recent cultural value, until I remembered some of the women of the Old Testament, women who kept their cool in circumstances that far exceeded any you and I face. Sarah's husband said she was his sister and then gave her to King Abimelech who put her in his harem to be prepared as his bride. Apparently, she did not by word or action betray that she was really Abraham's wife. Cool.

Or take Miriam, Moses' sister, after her mother had put the baby in an ark of tarred bulrushes. Miriam watched to see what would happen, saw the Pharaoh's daughter take the baby from the ark, and sauntered up to inquire if the princess might like a good nurse to care for the baby. Cool.

Or remember Esther, the Jewish queen of the Persian king. When she knew that all of her people might perish, she determined to do something about it, even if it meant losing her life. Her words: "If I perish, I perish." Cool.

Deborah, the judge of Israel, led a battle at the request of a man who was afraid to assume the leadership and said that he would go to battle only if she went with him. Her reply, "I will go with you. But because of the way you are going about this, the honor will not be yours, for the LORD will hand Sisera over to a woman" (Judges 4:9). Sisera was killed by a woman named Jael who tricked him into resting in her tent and then, after he was asleep, hammered a tent peg through his head. Cool. But cruel.

Cool doesn't necessarily mean right. But it does provide the mental setting in which you can think more clearly. Cool gives you time to react. Cool makes you more acceptable to the men you work for and with.

The Mentor Myth

In recent years, there have been certain passwords among working women—dressing for success, networking, and mentoring. While there is, of course, some truth in each of these, not one of them—not all of them together—will ensure success for anybody.

I haven't had the money to join the dress-for-success people, and you probably don't either. Women rather naturally understand networking, since they do it in so many areas of their lives. But the mentor matter is something else. A woman once informed me that she had told a certain executive in the company where I worked that he could be my mentor. Fortunately, he never started to "ment."

We all need to learn from others, but none of us needs one person who is the primary teacher/boss. It seems flattering to be sought out and coached by someone who is a bit older or higher in the company structure. And yet allowing yourself to be the "mentee" means that you are incurring debts, and debts have to be paid. You may feel so loyal that you are afraid to disagree with your mentor. You may forget that there are other ways of doing things and thus miss out on a course of action that would be better for you. You may neglect to look into your own evaluations of things. In a recent survey of working women, one-fifth of them said that they had been sleeping with their mentors. Some debt!

If you must have a mentor, make it a woman who is not your boss and put a mental time limit on the close relationship. Nothing hinders you more than to form an exclusive twosome. It can impair your judgment, interfere with your relationships, color your evaluation of what is happening around you, and it may blind you to your own potential.

The traditional system of mentoring implies that one of the parties is not quite grown up and that the other will be the parent figure. This often ends up as ego enrichment for the older one, while the younger person may play his or her own set of games. Not a healthy relationship.

You can learn so much from what you read—from books and magazines and newspapers. Magazines produced especially for the working woman give good information. I tried several others over a period of years and finally settled on *The Working Woman* as having the most balanced approach.

Self-Assessment

Decide what you want from work. What you want is going to change over the next years, but deciding what you are working toward will help. Right now, you may just want a regular paycheck and a place to work. That's fine. You can't manage big career aspirations when other parts of your life are clamoring for great amounts of attention. Still, it is important to have a job in which you feel comfortable, in which you see possibilities for advancement, and in which you feel competent. There will be plenty of time later to change direction, slightly or drastically.

Learn to assess your own strengths and weaknesses. Never underestimate the importance of good, periodic evaluations. Take them seriously, and let your boss know that you want to grow in your job competence. If testing is available, take advantage of it. Learn from your mistakes. Don't let them ground you, but rather sift out what you know to be true and improve your behavior where you can.

During the years since my divorce, work has been one of the most beneficial and restorative parts of my life. When it seemed that life had fallen apart, it was reassuring to go to the same place every day and know that I was doing something useful, that I was productive. It was good to have hours in which I was not confronted with the problems that filled the home and in which I could often forget my lowered status in life.

When I met two divorced women who had so much money that they didn't need to work, I envied them at first. But I slowly began to change my mind. They didn't seem to recover from divorce. They had nothing productive to do. No one needed them. They sat and wallowed in their money while I was running with my poverty. In the long run, I was far better off than they, and I gave thanks that I had had to work.

❦ Goals for Working

List short- and long-term goals for your career. Then list ways of working toward your goals.

Goals	What I Will Do
1. Education Goals	1.
2. Skills Development	2.
3. Achievement/Advancement	3.
4. Understanding	4.
5. Attitude	5.
6. Relationships	6.

CHAPTER SEVEN

NO STRANGER TO YOUR FEELINGS

God is here! God is acting! He is
changing emptiness to abundance.
Poverty to riches. Psychosis to sound
thinking. Bereavement to belonging.
Despair to delight. . . . But we must
obey in the face of our fears, for only
then can we behold the God
who acts.

—*Calvin Miller*

My God, permit me not to be a
stranger to myself and Thee.

—*Isaac Watts*

If you have felt outraged, afraid, trapped, hopeless, bitter, lonely, bored, meaningless, sad, inadequate, frantic, restless, unhappy, unloved—don't worry. You are normal. There would be something wrong with you if you could endure all the trauma of divorce and not have these feelings now and then.

The question is not *whether* you should feel this or that, but *what you are going to do* about the feelings as you look to the future. The danger is not in having the feelings. The danger is in *denying* negative feelings or acting as if they don't matter. They do matter, enormously, and your future emotional health depends on recognizing those feelings for what they are.

We think we are such rational beings. In church we may say, "Fact, not feeling," and even think we believe it—until the service is over and we get back to living.

Right now, your feelings are like ragged urchins, crying for care. At the same time, they seem like observers, separate from yourself. Because of this, it would be easy for you to violate them, to treat them with little respect, as if they were puffs of dandelion fur rather than the deep roots of your being. Yet if you ignore your feelings, you may end up a stranger to yourself and to God.

Your feelings are not observers—they are an important part of you. And what you are *aware* of feeling is probably only the tip of what is inside. You need to bring your feelings to the surface, to learn to respect them, and to express them in appropriate ways.

When life is in disarray, feelings seem to go in all directions at once. You find yourself reacting—and overreacting—to everything, until you no longer trust your own emotional stability. Don't write off your feelings. Instead, go deeper—down to the roots.

Our feelings are closely related to what we want and don't want, what we like and don't like. In fact, our lives are *shaped* by what we want, by our desires. When the apostle Peter wrote to the early Christians, he told them no longer to be shaped by evil desires. His implication was clear—they were shaped by their desires, but from that point on, they should be shaped by desires that would conform to the character of Christ being formed in them.

When you think of the one or two things in your life that you have wanted more than anything else, you probably can see them as threads of continuity in your experience. Those desires have shaped your thoughts and your behavior in more ways than you may want to admit.

When you now think about those desires in relation to God, and to the pain of divorce, you may feel anger at God for allowing what you cherished to have been so crushed. It took me a long time before I could even think about being angry at God, for after all, I was depending on him to get my children and me through our extreme need. How could I be angry at the very One who was holding us together?

Feelings are terribly complex, and they need our consistent attention. Please don't ignore your negative feelings. Don't feel guilty for having them. Rather, determine that you will learn to understand them, and that you will move toward control of feelings that are giving you trouble.

Outrage

You need to do something about your anger even though you have legitimate reason for it. Yes, your anger can be a motivator to high challenge and energetic action in the early months. But you need to make sure that each month, each year, your anger is lessening. Outrage that is not resolved, not detonated, can turn into bitterness, and bitterness will corrupt you and everyone around you.

Don't try to spiritualize your anger by saying it has all gone away when it hasn't. God understands better than you do that it would be unnatural *not* to react with anger at some of the things that have happened in your life. Even if there have been no barbaric acts, just the breaking of a marriage, the indignity of being left standing alone in the world, is enough to produce a good case of anger.

Seeing your children without a father makes you angry. Not having enough money makes you angry. Having to work intolerably long hours to survive exhausts and angers. Economic inequalities cause anger. The rejection of other people brings on anger. Having to deal with a total life change all at once produces anger.

Even so, most people don't like to be around angry divorced women. And this is where the danger of suppression comes in. You need people. You want to be acceptable. So, you may act as if you are not angry. And then you may believe it. The acting isn't a bad idea—just as long as you don't believe it. To work through the anger, the outrage, you need to understand and feel the extent of it.

Some types of anger are sinful, others are not. To be angry when someone else has caused heinous offense to one of your children is not a sin. But if you let that anger get out of control, if it leads you to revenge or keeps you awake at night and consumes your thoughts during the day, then it is a sin.

To feel anger at the breaking of a marriage is not a sin. But it can become sinful if you allow it to distort your approach to the future, if you let it lead you into bitterness.

Literature is full of angry women: Madame LeFarge in Dickens's *Tale of Two Cities*, Becky Sharp in Thackeray's *Vanity Fair*, Scarlett O'Hara of *Gone with the Wind*, and Medea, the spurned wife of Jason. In Euripedes' play, one of the characters says of Medea that she "will never learn to be humble, she will never learn to drink insult like harmless water . . . I say that poor people are happier; the little commoners and humble people, the poor in spirit; they can lie low under the wind and live while the tall oaks and cloud-raking mountain pine go mad in the storm, writhe, grown, and crash."

If you remember the play, you know that at the end, Medea, totally absorbed in her own tragedy, chooses to kill her two sons rather than let them go with their father. Blood dripping from her hands, she says to Jason: "You had love and betrayed it; now of all men you are utterly most miserable. As I of women. But I, as woman, despised, a foreigner alone, against you and the might of Corinth, have met you, throat for throat, evil for evil, vengeance for vengeance."

One of Medea's servants says to her, "O my lady . . . bend in this wind, and not be broken." That is good advice for an angry woman of today.[1]

Fear

Of course, you are afraid. You are having to risk so much in so many new ways all at once. You suddenly need knowledge and judgment you never needed before.

You are in a high-risk time, and you want to learn to use that fear to give you energy and nerve to do what must be done. Make the challenges work for you, and these years will be some of the most exciting and satisfying of your life, even in the midst of your loss and pain.

There is something energizing about necessity. I have done many things I would rather not have. Sometimes I was scared half to death, but I knew I had no choice—so I went ahead. My children were generally behind the necessity. If I had been alone, I might have been far less venturesome, far more reticent. And I would have gained much less.

Decide what is necessity for you. Don't subject yourself to undue stress by venturing into things that are not necessary. Save your energy for meeting needs.

You can alleviate some of your fear by effective planning, by seeking information that you need. There is no point in fearing the *unknown* when it is possible to *know*. And when it is *not* possible to know, fear is equally useless.

Most of the things people fear never happen. Don't waste your energy asking for trouble.

You will find yourself afraid in all sorts of situations. Listen to those fears, even if they seem insignificant or hard to understand. One night, at a picnic sponsored by a missions group, I discovered that the next item on the agenda was for all of us to tell what we had done since the last gathering. I left. I didn't know most of the people well, and I was not able, at that time, to say that I had been divorced during that time. I don't feel bad that I left. Talking in front of that group was not necessary, and it would have produced undue stress in me.

Respect yourself. You may have already gone off the top of the graph on the stress chart. Don't push yourself too far and risk getting sick. You and your children need you to be healthy.

Day by day and with each passing moment,
Strength I find to meet my trials here;
Trusting in my Father's wise bestowment,
I've no cause for worry or for fear.
He whose heart is kind beyond all measure
Gives unto each day what He deems best—
Lovingly, its part of pain and pleasure,
Mingling toil with peace and rest.

Day by Day and with Each Passing Moment

Choices

This book is about making choices. You are faced, as I was, with many individual decisions and with one all-important choice—whether to become who you appear to be or who you really are inside.

Which do you want more—to feel socially acceptable or to become more acceptable to yourself? Do you want to meet the surface role expectations of others more than you want to fulfill your own hopes and expectations?

You need to make a choice between appearance and reality, between the immediate and the delayed, between role satisfaction and inner development, between the quick fix and the long solution, between group approval and personal significance, between stagnation and growth, between placebos and real soul medicine.

How you feel about your own personal value will determine your decision. I hope you will choose for the long process, for the future. I hope you will decide in favor of what you believe God wants to do in you.

A choice that involves delay is especially hard for the divorced person because of the ragged emotions, the personal pain, the disruption of life, the loss of so many things. When you are grieving, it is natural to think there must be something that can take away your hurt. You see other people reaching for a placebo, and when it seems to help them, you are tempted to reach for one too.

Your feeling about your personal value will determine your choice. But there is more to it than that. You will choose growth rather than appearances if you feel that God is your loving Father who has long and good purposes for you, who is working in and around your life, even in this hard time, to bring good out of bad, life out of death. Did you notice the quotation from Calvin Miller at the beginning of this chapter? God is changing "bereavement to belonging, despair to delight . . . but we must obey in the face of our fears, for only then can we behold the God who acts."[2]

God's purposes are long and interrelated. If you are going to be a part of his purposes, you can't count on plugging in at any point you choose. You can't just push the celestial button and say, "Checking in, God. What great thing can I do for your kingdom today? Something that will win me instant success and wide approval, perhaps."

God uses prepared people—prepared within themselves, that is, so that they know him and know who they are in relation to him. God wants to act on your behalf. He does not want you to be a stranger to yourself or to him. Coming to know God, to know yourself, and to know his purposes, takes time. God is never in a hurry.

The choice before you is whether to go with God in faith to the land of promise or to insist on gratification now and probably miss the adventure.

This is what the LORD says:
"Stand at the crossroads and look;
ask for the ancient paths,
ask where the good way is, and walk in it,
and you will find rest for your souls."
—Jeremiah 6:16

If you have any sense of God calling you, then listen. God calls *all* Christians to holiness, peace, to evidencing the fruit of the Spirit, to spiritual disciplines, to finding their place in the body of Christ, to being involved in his redemptive work in the world.

In addition, we are each specially gifted—first at birth and then by the Holy Spirit after we become Christians. This means that we each have some sense of destiny, of calling, a feeling for what we could potentially do. If you want to find his potential for you, you need to get in step with him: listen, be quiet, know yourself, know his Word, pray, and then obey.

There is something wrong when professing Christians are on the same fast track as the rest of the world. I don't think God is in the fast lane. Nor is he well served by much that occurs there.

There is something wrong with spinning your wheels in frenetic activity that can never meet your inner needs. There is something wrong with investing exorbitant amounts of energy in what will not satisfy. It is rather like the question posed by the prophet Isaiah: "Why spend money on what is not bread, and your labor on what does not satisfy?" (Isaiah 55:2).

I know how easy it is to be tyrranized by the urgency of your own wants and emotional needs—so much so that you have a hard time thinking clearly. It is easy to fall into the syndrome of feeling that you have a right to be happy, that someone owes you something. But it's not so. God does not owe you a husband or an apology. Life does not owe you happiness. Rather, you will get what you go after. We have come full circle, back to the choice before you— for the immediate and easily gotten, or for growth, meaning, and true significance.

If you are unable to figure out your feelings, if you sense that they are working against you, and if you cannot make the kinds of choices you know you need to, consider seeking professional help. I also suggest three books by David Seamands that have been beneficial to many hurting people: *Healing for Damaged Emotions*, *Putting Away Childish Things*, and *Healing of Memories* (Wheaton, Ill.: Victor Books). These books will help you to determine whether you need counseling as you deal with your emotions, your memories, and your ability to make good choices for yourself and your children.

Retreat

Because you have been hurt, your self has a tendency to retreat, looking for protection. Common places for retreat are self-definition, self-absorption, and self-indulgence.

Self-definition

My problem was right here. I was forever trying to convince myself and God that *now* I understood. *Now* the process was over. *Now* I was ready. *Now* I had achieved the growth he desired. And *now* we could get on with things and forget this grinding discipline that seemed to continue forever.

Of course, you have to define yourself in this world. No one else is going to. But your definition in society should always be considered temporary—for today, transitional. When you stand before God, self-definition changes from your understanding to his, from your wishes to his will, from your short sight to his eternal vision. When you stand before God, the definition of your self is measured not merely by what you want and feel, but more significantly by what you can and will become. You are on your way to becoming *you.* The person you will someday be, on the other side, is so glorious as to make the present *you* seem a nobody. Yet that is not true, because the present you carries all the potential that will reside in the shining being you will be. And that potential, placed in you by God himself, can be and should be developed to a great degree in the years immediately ahead. For you are not to wait in limbo until the glory by and by. You are to live now in expectation, in hope—and that means being all that you can be right now.

Yes, it is natural to cling to narrow self-definitions. The unknown is frightening. Yet as you let go of your tight hold on self-definition, as you enter the silence and hear the stillness of God and see his holiness and let him touch the eyes of your soul, you will know that there is indeed hope and meaning and order ahead of you. You will experience God's care and love and know that he has not abandoned you. You are not an outcast to him. You are his loved child, and he is giving you the means of grace to become what he has in mind for you.

Yes, 'tis sweet to trust in Jesus,
Just from sin and self to cease;
Just from Jesus simply taking
Life and rest, and joy and peace.

Tis So Sweet to Trust in Jesus

Self-absorption

In Robert Lewis Taylor's *A Roaring in the Wind*, the main character, Ross Nickerson, is walking home one day thinking about his two friends, Grantly and James Duncan, and putting together what he knows of their background. And suddenly it occurs to him that he is a victim of self-absorbed parents.

What hurts children are given by self-absorbed parents! I thought with relief that I'd escaped all these, and was wrong. Ours was a family of generosity, concern, discipline. But no warmth or affection existed there; no single motherly hug, no fatherly pat on the back. Nothing but secret talks with my sister, who, I suddenly realized, would never be married, ever. She'd been treated, by my father, as a second son, and now shrank from any show of softness. I'd become aware of the reason I valued an occasional embrace by the Duncans. James, in lifting me off the floor, once brought a stab to my chest, and I'd never understood it till now.

Oh, well, I said aloud to the stars, Heaven save us from the curse of self-pity![3]

What is more natural than to go deep into yourself with your anger and your self-pity? And what is more harmful to you and to others?

Self-absorbed people often look as if they are operating from the best of motivations. They don't always seem selfish or mean, but they do appear truly to believe that the world centers on their hurts or their egos or their schedules or their fears. They can dominate households, ruin children, cause havoc in churches, and appear oblivious to what they are doing.

A self-absorbed woman refuses to give herself in depth to anyone and tries to hinder others from self-giving. She wants life to center on meeting her needs. A self-absorbed person manipulates and controls. She may see God as a simplistic deity who has little to do but listen to recitations of old hurts and fears. She may be in danger of becoming her own god, for all things do center on her. If she is her own golden calf, she offers occasional expiation for wrongs done to her so that she may be able to bear them.

What is the cure for self-absorption? Suffering. Pain worse than the person ever thought she could bear. Something to cut away the fatty tissue of self and get to the essence of personhood.

Have you been self-absorbed? And now you are suffering? Thank God for the pain you have experienced. Ask him to give you a clear view of yourself and your place in the world so that you can best serve him.

You can also be sure that more hurt will follow until the process is done. God is preparing you for his kingdom, and the kingdom is a place of touch—hand to hand, soul to soul. As God begins to pare down your oversized self, you will increasingly see your ability to act rather than merely react. You will begin to feel the Spirit move in you, and you will come to feel more free than you have for a long time.

Self-indulgence

The self-indulgers are the restless spenders. They overvalue things and sensations; they lavish all they can on themselves. They spend life extravagantly and savor every minute of it. And they are likely to feel alienated because of the distorted values they place on people and things. They are seeking wrong answers to legitimate questions. They are trying to solve emotional problems with material answers—and it won't work.

Their wrong evaluation of life puts them outside the normal pace of life. They have valued things more than people, pleasure more than purpose. They have valued their own ability to appreciate more than their ability to contribute.

Does this description sound familiar? Many people today are following this agenda. If you are one of them, consider the example of Christ, who willingly gave up his own pleasures to seek your good. Then surrender yourself and give disciplined obedience to God's purposes. Through this surrender and obedience, you will find yourself released to the service of others. For it is through deliberate service of those in need that you will learn the true meaning of things and people.

Your Need for Love

We all need to be touched. Some people claim that we need eight to ten hugs a day just to survive. But touch extends beyond the physical to the mental, emotional, and spiritual. People who live in close community are touched regularly by many people they feel close to. Those who live in the isolated nuclear family or alone place impossible expectations for touching and closeness on one or two people.

Do you feel that you just can't survive without a husband? If so, that's reason enough to make up your mind that you'll learn how. You can learn to stand up straight by yourself. You don't have to be in a perpetual leaning position. But standing up straight means learning to change the way you think about yourself.

Because you are in pain, you may assume that getting back into the role of wife will solve your problems. But what you need is not necessarily to become a *wife*—what you need is to be *healed*, to become everything you can be. Most people who choose for rapid remarriage are choosing a societal role rather than an intimate and mature relationship— and the divorce rate for early remarriages bears this out.

Realistically look at your own needs and aspirations. They may be hard to identify at times, blended as they are with role expectations. They are like Teilhard de Chardin's "indefinite fringes of reality." Yet where there is a fringe, there is a long thread. Follow this back to look at the weaving of your life. Find out who you are before you make any crucial decisions about the future.

One thing you will have to deal with is your attraction toward some of the men you know. Tell yourself early— and often, if necessary—that all the married ones are unavailable to you and that most of the single ones are unsuitable. Your emotions are telling you to find someone to lean on. Try to balance these emotions. You are in a precarious time, and you are a prime candidate for doing something stupid, to say nothing of hurtful.

In your associations with married men, place a fence around their marriages and determine never to violate them. This means, among other things, that you will be careful about the kinds of conversations you have with married men. Some people claim that talking is the most intimate human activity, and I tend to agree. Don't listen to complaints about a wife. Don't become emotionally dependent on a married male friend or allow him to become emotionally dependent on you. Keep a good friendship good.

Take it for granted that you will at times feel attracted to some of the men you see regularly. When you do, ask yourself why. Maybe he's physically attractive, clever, calm, accomplished—but there is probably something more than that involved. *What in you responds to this man?* Is it some part of your personality or potential that you have not yet worked to develop? Most likely, this man sees something in you that could be, that is not yet—and his seeing is helping you to see yourself in a new way.

Maybe what you are most attracted to is that part of yourself. This, after all, is one of the best gifts of friendship—this encouragement to become. And when you come to understand this aspect of friendship, you can then give thanks for good men who will challenge you and help you to grow.

We learn who we are from each other. We come to feel loved by the actions of many other people, and we should all be giving love every day. This love is not just marriage and sex. Love is the basis of friendship and human kindness. Love is the foundation of becoming.

When you see who I am, you encourage me to believe that I can reach a certain goal. While our encounter may be brief, you have invested love in me.

Christians especially need to encourage friendship between men and women—always, of course, preserving the sanctity of marriage. Many people do not know how to be friends with someone of the opposite sex. This inability affects their marriages, so that they do not enjoy friendship with their spouses. It makes them more vulnerable to sexual temptation, since they interpret every male-female encounter in a sexual context.

Jesus had friends who were women. He and his disciples traveled with a group of women who managed the practical needs of the group. His encounter with the woman at the well of Samaria allows us to listen in on a male-female conversation that was accepting, friendly, and so motivational that it changed her life. There was acceptance of her mental acuity. There was hope for her future. There was something special for her to do. There was forgiveness for her many sins. And there was a healing of relationships that reached into the life of her community. Jesus helped her to see herself in the context of who she could become. And this is precisely what friendships should do.

Learn to be a friend. Learn to maintain your friendships in an acceptable context in your church, community, and work place. You lose nothing worth having by keeping your behavior on the conservative side.

Your primary need right now is not for a husband. Your primary need is for you. It is for the affirming love and care that comes through relationships with men and women, children and old people, close friends and casual associates. For this, you need people. Lots of people. Someone has advised young people to acquire at least one hundred people who are part of their lives. He regards this as the only way to survive in today's rootless society. It is good advice for the divorced woman also.

Due Sense of Mercy

But I will sing of your strength,
in the morning I will sing of your love;
for you are my fortress,
my refuge in times of trouble.

—Psalm 59:16

I have kept a journal for many years, and I read through much of it in preparation for this book. I was surprised to find how often I was led to celebrate the love of God and to express praise. I wonder at this now, for I don't remember thanksgiving as such a significant part of those years. Yet in my dealings with the Lord, the praise was there, and I am more aware now of how essential it was—and is—to emotional healing and development.

I sometimes feel that I have nothing in particular for which to give thanks, just because I want so many things I don't have. If I stop and begin to list the things for which I *can* give thanks, it changes my whole outlook on life. The General Thanksgiving in the Anglican Prayerbook includes this wonderful petition:

> We beseech Thee, give us that due sense of all Thy mercies, that our hearts may be unfeignedly thankful; and that we show forth Thy praise, not only with our lips, but in our lives, by giving up ourselves to Thy service, and by walking before Thee in holiness and righteousness all our days, through Jesus Christ our Lord, to Whom, with Thee and the Holy Ghost, be all honor, and glory, world without end.

All of this petition hangs on the phrase "that due sense of all Thy mercies." The words "due sense" come to my mind so often. They refer not to what is due to me, but rather what is due to God. "Unfeignedly thankful" means sincerely so, without hypocrisy.

When you can discover what makes you glad, even in the most sorrowful situation, and when on the basis of that gladness you can order your life toward walking in holiness before God, you will know that you are not a stranger to yourself or to God.

❦ Feelings That Need Attention

List those feelings that most urgently need attention. Then prayerfully consider what you can do about them.

How I Feel	What I Will Begin to Do
1.	1.
2.	2.
3.	3.
4.	4.
5.	5.

CHAPTER EIGHT

SMALL DOSES OF SIGNIFICANCE

There is no point asserting and reasserting what the heart cannot believe.

—*Aleksandr I. Solzhenitsyn*

Ponder anew what the Almighty can do, if with His love He befriend thee.

—*Joachim Neander*

It is a question not merely of my being consoled but of my being completed.

—*Pierre Teilhard de Chardin*

What do you want more than anything else?

More than likely, the top item on your list has something to do with your need to feel significant. I am convinced that, more than anything else, people want a sense of significance—to know that they matter and that they figure in the scheme of things, on a personal and community level.

You might think that we carry most of these feelings of significance within ourselves, but we don't. They are largely granted to us by other people. We acquire them by reflection.

As young children, we learned who we were by the mirrors we saw in the eyes and in the responses of family members. Those reflections were reinforced over the years as we moved into larger spheres of living.

In *Healing for Damaged Emotions*, David Seamands talks about family mirrors:

Do you remember the last time you went into the house of mirrors in an amusement park? You looked in one mirror and saw yourself as tall and skeletal, with foot-long hands. In the next one, you were round like a big balloon. Another mirror combined both, so that from the waist up you looked like a giraffe, while from the waist down you looked like a hippopotamus.

Looking into the mirrors was a hilarious experience, especially for the person standing next to you. He was just knocked out at how funny you looked. What was happening? The mirrors were so constructed that you saw yourself according to the curvature of the glass.

Now, move those mirrors over into the family. What if somehow your mother, your dad, your brother, your sister, your grandparents, the important others in your early life—what if they had taken every mirror in the house and curved them a certain way, so that in every mirror you saw a distorted reflection of yourself? What would have happened?

It wouldn't have taken you long to develop an image of yourself just like the one you were seeing in the family mirrors. After a while, you would have begun talking and acting and relating to people in a way that would have fit the picture you kept seeing in those mirrors.[1]

You know what these distorted reflections are like. You have lived with them for some time in your home, and you probably are still carrying some distortions from your past. Right now, as a divorced person, you are experiencing rejection or indifference or misunderstanding that make it very hard for you to feel significant.

You want to stand tall and straight before the mirrors, yet you feel crouched in a most unattractive position. You want to look good and virtuous, but you keep seeing blemished reflections in the eyes of others. You want to be understood in your actions and motives, but you feel as if people are forcing you to wear a sign. You look in the mirror and see a label in front of your face. You want to be loved and cherished, but there is no one to love you.

You wish to reflect a unity of personhood, yet you sense a profound disagreement between your inner feelings and your outer acts, to say nothing of the disagreement between what you are inside and others' perceptions of you. You want to feel independent and proud, in a good sense. Yet you occasionally feel forced to stoop to the indignity of words and actions that seem far beneath you.

Even in the best of times, your inner person longs to be seen and recognized for who you most surely are; yet you also want concealment. Your inner person wants expression; yet you also pull back. Because of the confusion of personal identity deep within, because of the distorted mirrors in your life, it would be easy for you to ignore that person inside of you.

You need to do two things for your inner self. First, move toward a coordination of your inner self and the outer expression of who you are so that *you* agree with *you*. Second, move toward expressions of your selfhood that will offer you genuine feelings of significance. If you choose not to work on these two aspects of your life, you condemn yourself to misery.

The narrator of Albert Camus' *The Fall* is a man who felt that he lived a double existence. Then he was condemned to existence in an ancient and confining prison:

> I had to live in the little-ease. To be sure, you are not familiar with that dungeon cell that was called the little-ease in the Middle Ages. In general, one was forgotten there for life. That cell was distinguished from others by ingenious dimensions. It was not high enough to stand up in nor yet wide enough to lie down in. One had to take on an awkward manner and live on the diagonal; sleep was a collapse, and walking a squatting, *Mon cher*, there was genius—and I am weighing my words—in that so simple invention. Every day through the unchanging restrictions that stiffened his body, the condemned man learned that he was guilty and that innocence consists in stretching joyously.[2]

You too know what it is like to live in little-ease. The very notion that you can stand up straight may seem to be nonsense. And yet you don't want to stay in such a confined position.

How do you get out of this mental and emotional enclosure? By choosing the kinds of significance you want to achieve in the coming years and by deciding how you will go about finding it. As you consider this, remember that significance comes in small doses, just as reflections in mirrors come to us a glance at a time.

What Makes You Feel Significant?

You feel significant when your inner self and your outer self agree.

You feel significant when important people in your life see who you truly are and value you for your selfness.

You feel significant when you know it is all right to express your deepest emotions and needs.

You feel significant when you begin to achieve long-held ambitions.

You feel significant when you know you are learning to manage your life in harmony with the needs of your own soul, with the skills you have learned, and the demands of people close to you.

You feel significant when you can deeply reach to the selfness of another person with a caring, healing touch.

You feel significant when you take large risks to gain something you want very much.

This need for significance—where does it come from? Long before you were born, the image of God was printed on your inner self, and it is this that makes you truly human, with all the potential glory of what that can mean.

The image of God stamped on your individuality, wanting to be expressed in your developing personality—this is sacred and sublime. Yet this image of God is too often ignored in home, church, and certainly in society at large. The image of God within you always votes for your own unity of self and for the peace of inner and outer expression. Yet its vote may never be heard in the confusion of destructive behaviors that make up the life around you. Still, that vote, the voice within, will not be silent, for the image of God within you keeps alive an insistence on what your heart can believe. It keeps alive an impatience with the assertions that your heart can never believe. And you look and you wait for the person, the few people, who can see who you truly are.

Granted, these mirror reflections of you are bound to be hazy, for that is the nature of life. The apostle Paul said it this way, "Now we see in a mirror dimly." And that is all you can expect in this world. And yet the inevitability of less-than-clear reflections should not deter you from striving to see ever more clearly or from giving to others as well-defined an image of who they are as is possible.

But back to the question—where do we find significance? Most of us have compartmentalized lives, so that we see one set of people at work, another at home, another at church, another in a leisure pursuit. And this means that we need to achieve significant interchanges in each of these arenas of our lives.

Home

The most important people to you in your home are your children. As you continue to be a responsible and caring parent, you will experience the satisfaction of doing what is good and right for them. And they should come to appreciate you deeply, treating you not as a plaster saint but as a loved parent and friend.

About eighteen months after my divorce, I received from my daughter a letter that I treasure. She was home from college for a weekend, and just before she went back, she wrote this note and left it for me:

> It's quiet . . . the first few minutes I've been alone while I've been home. It's good to have these minutes to reflect, this time at home. The Lord has been ever so good to us, Mom. A few times while I've been home, I've just wanted to put my arms around you and cry . . . Maybe you don't want pity though . . . although I guess it is not pity exactly because I trust the Lord, our Father, to continue His generosity and love and care for you. Mom, I love you.

After some words of advice about her brother, she wrote:

Don't back down, or be "too nice." The greatest proof I have that you loved and love me is that you set boundaries for me to grow up in. In a world full of abstracts and indefinite answers, you had some answers, even it if was no. Even the no's gave me a security that there was a person who cared enough to back me up against a wall and lay down the law.

Mom, thank you for all you've done to make this a special weekend. I hope as I move more and more into my womanhood that we will become good friends and grow more in understanding and appreciating our differences.

I love you . . . Mommie.

Respect your children. Help them to visualize themselves in the future. As you look deeply into who they are and affirm the person deep within them, you will encourage them toward the unity of person so necessary for their own feelings of significance. And they will love and bless you for it. They do not have to be just like you. They do need to be faithful to who they are deep inside. There is no point in your asserting and reasserting what their hearts cannot believe. Learn to speak the truth of authenticity to who they are.

Work

You may see your work colleagues more than you see any other group, including your family. For this reason, it is important that you have work experiences that make you feel significant. These will result from meeting your own personal goals, from your understanding of competence joined with the way your boss understands it, and also from personal relationships that affirm you.

I assume that you will have work friends who are women. I urge you also to make friends with some of the men you work with. You have a special need of male friends in this time of reconstruction.

I have worked with many men, coworkers in the office and authors I would see occasionally. When I began working, I was so bruised inside that I had difficulty responding with grace to *any* man. I overreacted or underreacted or was defensive. I didn't have that ease that is so key to a good working partnership. And I owe much to some good men who showed patience and kindness.

I believe that women come to know who they are in relationship with men—and men with women. I needed the friendship, the encouragement, the fun and lightness of conversation, the affirmation, the belief in me that these men showed. I needed their mirror reflections to value myself properly. I needed these small doses of significance so that I could grow and become.

The small doses came in ordinary settings, and the fact that they were ordinary made them even more meaningful. It was not as if someone said, "What can we do about Carole?" Rather, the men were acting within the regular routines of their lives and giving me affirmation at the same time.

It is important that you have friendships in your work world—not only with men, of course, but certainly not excluding them, either. But do remember what you are at work for—you work for goals that you and your employer share. The side benefits of friendship are a plus for both you and your employer.

Church

When I was young, church was a place of special significance for me, as it has been for most of the years of my adult life. But at the time of my divorce, I found the church I was in to be of no real help; in fact, I felt myself distinctly unwelcome. What made this especially hard is that it was the church I grew up in.

I changed churches and got into a better situation. But the matter of church and significance was the one element of my life that went largely unresolved for several years. I wonder, in fact, whether there *is* an adequate answer for the divorced woman.

People have different needs, and one of mine was to be in a church that did not segregate single and divorced people. I never attended singles' groups; however, if you want to be part of such a group, do evaluate the program before you get too far into it. Determine whether higher emphasis is placed on growth and learning and service than on social potential. A church that sponsors a group that is little more than a mutual commiseration society or a dating pool helps no one. Sometimes I think that such groups are for comfort of the married people in the church who want to enclose all the previously marrieds in one room and hope they come out two by two.

This question of remarriage is very difficult for most pastors and churches to deal with. Some churches solve it by refusing ever to marry divorced persons. If they combine this position with a ministry of healing and growth, they can provide real benefits. After all, the divorced people who are part of a church like that are certainly not there for the marriage possibilities, so they're probably there because of spiritual dedication. If divorced people are given opportunities to serve in and through the church, many of them will minister with a compassion that reflects their own experience with God and with an accepting and loving church.

Those churches that marry divorced people may run into greater problems, partly because most of them perform the marriages whenever the divorced persons feel they're ready—and this is potentially dangerous. The percentage of failure for second marriages is higher than for first marriages.

A church that does marry divorced people should set a time limit—no remarriage for five years after the divorce. By this time, most of these people will have had time to solve their personal traumas. They will have had time to learn how to live alone and stand up straight all by themselves. The chances are much better that they are marrying for the right reasons.

In the first year after my divorce, I needed the church. I needed a pastor to come into our home and, in a sense, bring the presence and care of the church to us in our new setting. I would so much have liked to have a house blessing during those first months, but there was no one I could ask to do this. The pastor I had been in touch with before the divorce moved to a church across the country. There was no point in asking someone who had showed no care for us at all. In fact, from the church we were in at that time, no staff person or official caller ever came to our apartment until they had a fund drive, about two years later. They didn't care about us, but they did want our pledge of money for an expensive new building. As you might imagine, I wasn't inclined to give.

The church has experienced a terrible breakdown in pastoral care in the last generation. It used to be that when a pastor had three hundred people in his church, he believed he could call on his parishioners regularly. Now when a pastor has nine hundred parishioners and two or three assistants, he believes he can't call.

But a pastor can learn from home calls some things he just can't learn in any other way. He can gain a feel for how a family or person lives—things that never could be transmitted verbally. Yet we have a generation of clergy—certain small groups excepted—that does not know how to minister on a personal level, except when it is too late to do much except console. Why has this happened? Harold Ivan Smith suggests one reason: "Somehow, too many servants become lost in the politics of the church—and no denomination or independent work is immune . . . Increasingly, success in the ordained ministry is determined by the nonpriestly functions. The pastor has emerged as manager."[3]

I continue to hope that more pastors will come to understand the terrible isolation of the Christian divorced person. Most of the gestures toward adjustment should be made by the church, rather than leaving everything to the person who already feels like an outsider, a failure, and a misfit.

How is this to be done? People going through divorce experience similar stages and feelings, and they need certain things to help them cope with those stages. No pastor can be expected to remember what this woman or that man needs next week. But the church can set up a process for caring for divorced or widowed people. Pastors can put the names of such people on their calendars, anticipating needs that may arise during certain months (such as, this need in April, that need in June, and something else in August). Pastors can then plan ways that either they or some other sensitive person in their congregation can work to meet the needs of these hurting people.

Most pastors are probably uncomfortable with the way they deal with divorced people. And because they don't know what to do, they often do nothing. And yet it isn't all that difficult to find out what needs doing.

I believe in the church. I believe that it is the body of Christ on this earth, for all of its imperfections. But I have had a hard time with the church in these years because it has a changed meaning for me now. In my present church, I have had ample opportunity to serve; yet I often feel as though I don't belong. Part of that feeling, I'm sure, comes because I have a hard time accepting being divorced. I find I don't fit gracefully into that category. You may not either.

I encourage you not to use divorce as an excuse for not attending. Get yourself there regularly. Contribute regularly. Find a place to serve. Your feelings aren't the gauge of whether you should be part of the visible body of Christ. As a Christian, you are to be a responsible member of a local group of believers. You are not given other options.

Friends

You need friends, even though you may not have much time to see them. But be prepared for changes in relation to your friends. Before the divorce, I had been part of a weekly prayer group, and I assumed that the women in that group would be a support base for me. I was wrong. The few who retained feelings of friendship were those who had been friends in a personal way long before. I thought that certain friends who entertained a great deal would include me in some of their groups.

A few people will offer their friendship to you, and you may feel somewhat dependent on them for a time. One day in that awful year before the divorce, when I was in turmoil emotionally and in need of even the smallest dose of significance, a friend called me at work to ask if she could bring some lunch and if we could go to a park nearby and eat together. I was so moved by what she did and the grace of her spirit—completely out of sync with what I was encountering elsewhere—that I wrote these lines:

A friend, a good Samaritan, came on a sunny spring day, with a beautiful lunch on a tray, with linen placemats and napkins, lotus bowls filled with salad of chicken and fruit and nuts, some hot rolls and herb tea and cookies.

She came with quiet gracious love, not preaching, not judging, not analyzing, not applying bandaids to a cancer.

She didn't even bring up the sore subject, I did, and then she said she would talk about it only if I wanted to.

She came free of fear. I had seen so much fear in that long year.

I asked her why she was not afraid as everyone else seemed to be.

She explained that she had been hurt badly as a child. I said that most people had been hurt at some time. And she replied, "Yes, but most of them have never learned anything from the hurt. And so they are still afraid."

She felt my pain. She knew how bad it was, and she made no ridiculous suggestions about how to revive a dead marriage. No pious words about, "Be strong." Instead she spoke of my children and my grandchildren-to-be and of the sacrifices that are sometimes necessary to promote the moral strength of succeeding generations. She talked of the inheritance we shared in Christ, of glory, of life beyond, of hurts, of power that drew a dead Christ back to life.

And somewhere in her gracious ways and beautiful lunch and noble words, I saw Him standing there, and I heard His call—"Carole, Carole, you hurt so much. Give Me all of this, all the pain, all the impossibilities, all the reasons—not part but all of it."

This dear friend, Pauline Parker, became my daughter's mother-in-law in 1982. She and her husband, Dr. Paul Parker, are part of my extended family.

It is a sound principle of relationship that we need to invest our emotional energy in the direction of the people who nurture us. Why, then, is it so easy for divorced people to ignore and thereby devalue those friends who stick by us, to expend time and energy in wishful thinking, in hoping, in pursuing attractions to new faces? Probably it's because most divorced people really want to be married, want to be thought of as married, want to enjoy the status in society given to married people. Some of us will go to great lengths to escape the category of the divorced. And that feeling does not help us cherish people who are trying to be friends.

Another reason is that so many divorced people are angry—at individuals and at the world in general. Unfortunately, this anger is sometimes unleashed on those who have done nothing to cause the hurt. Friends, for instance. They seem safe. They don't seem to matter as much as those distant people who offended. This irrational behavior puts the divorced person in a double bind—they've lost the people who inflicted the pain, and now they may lose those who are trying to help restore them.

It is important to me to have reasonably normal social contacts—meaning, in part, that I don't see only women. That's one reason I became part of a once-a-month discussion group that includes several people I have known for a long time, most of them married.

Even though my time to spend with friends has not been as much as I would have liked, it is in this area of my life that I have felt the small doses of significance continually applied, year after year. It is here I have experienced the healing balm of the long contact with the people I do see, some from each of the several segments of my life. Although it is not an option for everyone, travel has given me the opportunity to renew old friendships and make new ones.

Self-appreciation

I give myself doses of significance as I come to understand myself better and to see and appreciate my growth and development. I have learned that I need to be fairly generous with myself, that I need to love myself in the same way I would extend love to anyone else, that I need to be patient, caring, and kind to myself.

I need to applaud myself when I do something difficult for the first time. I need to give myself credit for growing and becoming and changing.

I need to pursue some of the things that make me feel good, like working with color, decorating, going to plays, listening to good music, reading, and writing.

When I know that I have done something especially expressive of myself, I need to recognize that and promise to move in the same direction again soon.

I need to believe that I am worth the notice of other people and then receive their care and attention when it is given. I also need to feel free to ask for their help. And that is not particularly easy to do, if I don't feel all that worthy.

I feel significant when I know that I am increasingly taking charge of my life and making good things happen because I want them to. This was not easy for me in the first couple of years.

I feel significant when I know that I have made a good decision.

I feel significant in a minor way when I know that I look nice.

I feel significant when I have personal interchanges that go beyond the surface and reach deeply into who we both are. I feel significant when I can meet another person's need in a way that has some risk—and also when I receive warm thanks from that person.

I feel significant when I can figure out the meaning of something complicated going on around me or within me or both.

All of these things, though small happenings, give me significance—in small doses. They are effective for me because I have tried to determine what it is I want, what I like, what I need. You too need to find out what satisfies you, what warms your heart, what makes you feel significant.

The Importance of the Small

In the summer of 1971, our family went to Alaska to live for one year. In the vastness of space around us, in great distances to the next mountain peak, in broad expanses filled with wildflowers or blueberries and lowbush cranberries, in a land with so few people, in our little house with our rationed supply of water, I learned something about the importance of the small. In a land of wild animals and frozen winters, human life could continue because of small places of shelter, small acts of caring, small but detailed attention to the equipment and communication systems on which we all depended. Or a small provision of Alaska law, for instance, that made it illegal to pass a car stopped on the highway.

And my attention was drawn to God's words to the prophet Zechariah, "Who despises the day of small things?" (Zechariah 4:10).

When Elijah was seeking the Lord at Mount Horeb, he saw the earthquake and the fire, but the Lord was not in them. Rather, he was in a still small voice. When Jesus fed the people, he began with a few small fish. To supply our constant need for water, God "maketh small the drops of water" (Job 36:27, KJV), so that they will not destroy what they are intended to nourish.

Right now you want major repairs in your life, and you may find yourself losing patience with the small, day-by-day ordinaries that make up a life. But you'll probably never see the major repairs if you don't appreciate the small goodnesses of your life.

You also may find yourself becoming bored with what is happening around you. It's not what you want, or it seems insignificant compared with the major changes you have recently experienced. Boredom with the commonplaces of your life can be a real enemy of growth and peace. You can come to feel like Alice in Wonderland who "had got so much into the way of expecting nothing but out-of-the-way things to happen, that it seemed quite dull and stupid for life to go on in the common way."[4]

Pay attention to the way you are responding to the changes in your life as well as to the kind of expectations you place on yourself. If you often find yourself feeling bored, do something about it—in small ways. Don't catapult yourself into yet another major change, just because you are tired of your routines.

On the other hand, don't view your present life condition as permanent. It isn't, unless you see it that way. You are a person on your way to wholeness. You are recovering; you are reconstructing your life. If you have to put up with some boredom now and then, just put up with it—or think of creative ways to use the time.

Suffering

"There is no point asserting and reasserting what the heart cannot believe." The heart will seem to believe all sorts of untrue things, as long as they don't matter. But when the pressure is on, when it matters more than anything else in the world, the heart will believe only what it knows to be true.

Nobody wants to suffer. Yet everybody does. It just comes to us in different forms. Because so many people don't learn much from their pain, great amounts of nonsense have been spoken and written about it. Don't believe what you know in your heart is not true.

I have come to believe that suffering is one of the necessary works for the Christian because it seems to be God's way of purifying us. While God does not cause our troubles, he is with us in them, to "sanctify to us our deepest distress," as the hymn says. And looking at the sheer economics of suffering, it is a waste to go through all that pain and not be any better for it—not be any more prepared to help someone else who is hurting, not any more deeply understand what God is trying to teach us.

I have little sympathy for professional sufferers. The continual groaners. The people who tell you far more than you ever want to know about their troubles—most of which aren't worth mentioning.

Your problems are real enough. And they are not going to be over in a month or a year. In this time of real distress, you have the special opportunity to behave with dignity and grace and some humor.

You have the chance to stand tall, even when you don't feel like it. You have the blessed opportunity to learn more of what it means to be indwelt by the Spirit of Christ. The Holy Spirit does not turn you into a superwoman, but he does give you continuing strength and endurance and wisdom and grace.

One of the symbols of the Holy Spirit is oil. In biblical times, oil was poured into wounds. I don't have to tell you that you are wounded. You know that all too well. I knew I had wounds too, and I was afraid that I would bear permanent scars. I didn't want to be maimed, disfigured, scarred.

It took me a while to accept that it was in those scars that the grace of God was being especially applied to my life. I then had to decide whether I was willing to let that grace be extended to other people from the very scarred places or whether I would forever try to hide them and hold the goodness to myself.

I had to decide, really, whether I thought I was better than Jesus at this point. For he acquired scars for the faults of others and he still bears them. After his resurrection, the proof of his identity was not his voice, not his power to work miracles, not his appearance, not his teaching, but his scars.

Even though the New Testament speaks of our suffering with Christ, not many Christians aspire to this. We rarely hear about the work of suffering for Christ or with Christ. Once in a while we find a reference to Paul's prayer, "That I may know him, and the power of his resurrection, and the fellowship of his sufferings, being made conformable unto his death" (Phil. 3:10, KJV).

Yet Paul also wrote: "If we suffer, we shall also reign with him" (2 Tim. 2:12, KJV). "The Spirit himself testifies with our spirit that we are God's children. Now if we are children, then we are heirs—heirs of God and co-heirs with Christ, if indeed we share in his sufferings in order that we may also share in his glory" (Romans 8:16-17).

And Peter wrote, "To this you were called, because Christ suffered for you, leaving you an example, that you should follow in his steps . . . And the God of all grace, who called you to his eternal glory in Christ, after you have suffered a little while, will himself restore you and make you strong, firm and steadfast" (1 Peter 2:21, 5:10).

The New Testament seems to take suffering for granted. If Christ suffered, we shall also.

The prophet Isaiah wrote of the suffering of the people of God: "Do not fear, for I am with you; do not be dismayed, for I am your God. I will strengthen you and help you; I will uphold you with my righteous right hand" (Isaiah 41:10).

"When you pass through the waters, I will be with you; and when you pass through the rivers, they will not sweep over you. When you walk through the fire, you will not be burned; the flames will not set you ablaze" (Isaiah 43:2).

As you deal with God about your wounds, your scars, your losses, be completely honest with him, for only in this honesty will you find him to be your answer, your Word for life, your way, your comfort. "How can Christ sanctify fantasy? The creative processes of the Holy Spirit that bring God's power are fully operative only when we admit exactly where we are, only when we own our failures as well as our successes. One of the abiding glories of the Gospel is that it brings us face to face with reality about ourselves and the world."[5]

The Book of Isaiah speaks much about a woman afflicted. Chapters 40–66 voice comfort for the woman, Jerusalem, who has suffered. Each time I read chapters 40–52, I sense the anticipation building—the King is coming. In chapter 52, the woman is told to get ready, to dress herself for the one who will shortly arrive—when, abruptly, she comes face to face with that King as the Suffering Servant. She doesn't want to look, and yet there is no way for her to reach the kingdom realities of the later chapters of Isaiah without confronting the Suffering Messiah, whom we see especially in Isaiah 53.

You too need to confront the suffering Christ. For as you do and as you allow him to comfort and strengthen you, you will learn what it means to suffer as a Christian. Nothing can offer you deeper feelings of significance than for the Lord of Creation and Redemption to come alongside you and humbly show you his wounds, quietly identify himself with you in your pain, and then graciously permit you to be identified with him in his.

This is meaning beyond any earthly definition of that word. It connects all that you are with all that you ever will be. For as you learn how to live with both your deepest desires and your most agonizing pain and loss, you grow strong in a way you didn't know was possible. And you become ever more thankful for the grace that surrounds your days, not to insulate you from hurt, but to enable you to become all that you *hope* you can be and that God *knows* you can be.

You have made known to me the path of life;
you will fill me with joy in your presence,
with eternal pleasures at your right hand.

—Psalm 16:11

❦ Choices for Significance

What Makes Me Feel Significant	What I Will Choose to Do
1.	1.
2.	2.
3.	3.
4.	4.
5.	5.
6.	6.

AFTERWORD

Y ou don't want to stay on the wounded list any longer than necessary. You want to move toward healing and normalcy.

When Victor Frankl was freed from a concentration camp at the end of World War II, he experienced the release from suffering in this way:

> Larks rose to the sky and I could hear their joyous song. There was nothing but the wide earth and sky and the larks' jubilation and the freedom of space. I stopped, looked around, and up to the sky—and then I went down on my knees. At that moment there was very little I knew of myself or of the world—I had but one sentence in mind—always the same: "I called to the Lord from my narrow prison and He answered me in the freedom of space."[1]

You too may have felt confined to a narrow prison, to the little-ease of which Camus wrote. But you are not meant to live that way for long. God will answer you also in the freedom of space, in an ever-widening place of stretching joyously, where you can extend the oil of his healing balm to someone else who is wounded and afraid—but open to his love.

NOTES

Chapter 3

1. Arnold Prater, *Release from Phoniness* (Waco, Tex.: Word Books, 1968), 20.

Chapter 4

1. Pat Lagerkvist, *The Marriage Feast and Other Stories* (London: Chatto and Windus, 1967), 12-13, 29.
2. Richard J. Foster, *Celebration of Discipline* (New York: Harper & Row Publishers, 1978), 24.
3. Henry Nouwen, *The Wounded Healer* (Garden City, N.Y.: Doubleday & Company, Inc., 1972), 91-93.
4. Josef Pieper, *Leisure: The Basis of Culture* (New York: New American Library, 1963), 41.

Chapter 5

1. Joan Beck, *Chicago Tribune,* 2 May 1984.
2. Marie Winn, *Children Without Childhood* (New York: Pantheon Books, 1983), 4, 6-7.
3. Brian Stiller, *A Generation Under Siege* (Wheaton, Ill.: Victor Books, 1983), 20.
4. Ross Campbell, *How To Really Love Your Teenager* (Wheaton, Ill.: Victor Books, 1982), 10.

Chapter 7

1. *Man in Literature* (Glenview, Ill.: Scott, Foresman and Company, 1970), 86-87, 121, 91.

2. Calvin Miller, *The Taste of Joy* (Downers Grove, Ill.: InterVarsity Press, 1983), 137.
3. Robert Lewis Taylor, *A Roaring in the Wind* (New York: Putnams, 1978), 198.

Chapter 8

1. David A. Seamands, *Healing for Damaged Emotions* (Wheaton, Ill.: Victor Books, 1981), 62.
2. Albert Camus, *The Fall* (New York: Vintage Books, 1956), 109-110.
3. Harold Ivan Smith, *Tear Catchers* (Nashville: Abingdon Press, 1984), 66.
4. Lewis Carroll, *Alice's Adventures in Wonderland* (London: Cathay Books, 1983), 23.
5. Kent Hughes, *Behold the Man* (Wheaton, Ill.: Victor Books, 1984), 167.

Afterword

1. Victor Frankl, *Man's Search for Meaning* (New York: Pocket Books, 1963), 142.

Additional Resources

Books:

Bangley, Bernard. *If I'm Forgiven, Why Do I Still Feel Guilty?* Wheaton, Ill.: Harold Shaw Publishers, 1992.

Barnes, Robert G., Jr. *Single Parenting: A Wilderness Journey.* Wheaton, Ill.: Tyndale House Publishers, 1984.

Bertolini, Rebecca. *Mom's Big Activity Book for Building Little Characters.* Wheaton, Ill.: Victor Books/Scripture Press, 1992.

Brock, Anita. *Divorce Recovery.* Fort Worth, Tex.: Star Publications, 1991 reprinted.

Burkett, Larry. *The Complete Financial Guide for Single Parents.* Wheaton, Ill.: Victor Books/Scripture Press.

Capehart, Jody. *Cherishing and Challenging Children: Practical Tips for Parenting with Creativity and a Tender Heart.* Wheaton, Ill.: Victor Books/Scripture Press, 1992.

Dettoni, John, and Carol Dettoni. *Parenting Before and After Work.* Wheaton, Ill.: Victor Books/Scripture Press, 1992.

Divorce Recovery for Teenagers. Zondervan Publishing House, 1990.

Diamond, Susan A. *Helping Children of Divorce: A Handbook for Parents and Teachers.* New York: Schocken, 1986.

Hart, Archibald D. *Children and Divorce: What to Expect, How to Help.* Waco, Tex.: Word Books, 1982.

Johnson, Laurene, and Georglyn Rosenfeld. *Divorced Kids: What You Need to Know to Help Kids Survive a Divorce.* Nashville: Thomas Nelson Publishers.

Krementz, Jill. *How It Feels When Parents Divorce.* New York: Alfred A. Knopf, 1988.

Lieberman, Joseph I. *Child Support in America: Practical Advice for Negotiating and Collecting a Fair Settlement*. New Haven and London: Yale University Press, 1988.

Mastison, Judith. *Divorce—the Pain and the Healing: Personal Meditations When Marriage Ends*. Minneapolis: Augsburg Fortress Books, 1985.

Minar, Barbra. *Close Connections: Creatively Loving Those Nearest You*. Wheaton, Ill.: Victor Books/Scripture Press, 1992.

_____. *Unrealistic Expectations*. Wheaton, Ill.: Victor Books/Scripture Press, 1990.

Minirth, Frank, Paul Meier, and Don Hawkins. *Worry-Free Living*. Nashville: Thomas Nelson Publishers, 1989.

Peppler, Alice Stolper. *Single Again—This Time with Children*. Minneapolis: Augsburg Fortress Books, 1982.

Peterson, Judy. *Something of Your Own: Your Personal Journey to a Meaningful and Satisfying Life Work*.

Porter, Jane. *Parenting Alone: A Network Discussion Guide*. Wheaton, Ill.: Harold Shaw Publishers, 1992.

Seamands, David A. *Healing for Damaged Emotions*. Wheaton, Ill.: Victor Books/Scripture Press, 1981.

_____. *Healing Grace*. Wheaton, Ill.: Victor Books/Scripture Press, 1988.

_____. *Healing of Memories*. Wheaton, Ill.: Victor Books/Scripture Press, 1985.

_____. *Putting Away Childish Things*. Wheaton, Ill.: Victor Books/Scripture Press, 1982.

Sedgwick, Carolyn. *When Mothers Must Work*. Springdale, Penn.: Whitaker House, 1988.

Virkler, Henry A. *Speaking Your Mind Without Stepping on Toes: A Christian Approach to Assertiveness*. Wheaton, Ill.: Victor Books/Scripture Press, 1991.

Organizations

American Home Business Association
397 Post Road
Darien, CT 06820

Big Brothers and Big Sisters of America
National headquarters 230 North 13th St., Philadelphia, PA 19107-1510. Telephone: 215/567-7000.
This agency maintains lists of local agencies working with children from single-parent homes.

Homeworkers Organized for More Employment
P.O. Box 10
Orland, ME 04472

Mothers At Home
P.O. Box 2208
Merrifield, VA 22116
This organization publishes a magazine, *Welcome Home,* and offers other publications and a speakers' bureau. Many professional women find this group helpful for making the transition from job to home.

Mothers' Home Business Network
P.O. Box 423
East Meadow, NY 11554

New Ways to Work
149 Ninth Street
San Francisco, CA 94103

Parents Without Partners
National headquarters 8807 Colesville Rd., Silver Spring, MD 20910. Telephone 301/588-9354.
This organization is the largest devoted to the welfare and interests of single parents and their children. The group publishes *The Single Parent* magazine and other resource materials. For a Divorce Bibliography for Parents send $.50 to the above address.